JAPA YOGA

JAPA YOGA

SIR SWAMI SIVANANDA

GYAN

Published by

Gyan Publishing House
5, Ansari Road
Daryaganj, New Delhi-110002
Phone: 011-47034999, 9811692060
E-mail: books@gyanbooks.com

Distribution Network
gyanbooks.com
India, USA, Canada, UK, Australia

ISBN: 978-93-6920-689-6 (PB)

First Published, 1942

2nd Impression 2025

Printed at: Gyan Press, Delhi.

JAPA YOGA
Author: SIR SWAMI SIVANANDA

JAPA YOGA

JAPA YOGA

A COMPREHENSIVE TREATISE ON
MANTRA-SASTRA

Sri Swami Sivananda

Dedicated

To

Devarshi Narada, Dhruva, Prahlada, Valmiki, Tukaram, Ramdas, Sri Ramakrishna and all Yogis who realised God through the Divine Name

SRI SWAMI SIVANANDA

Born on the 8th September, 1887, in the illustrious family of Sage Appayya Dikshitar and several other renowned saints and savants, Sri Swami Sivananda had a natural flair for a life devoted to the study and practice of Vedanta. Added to this was an inborn eagerness to serve all and an innate feeling of unity with all mankind.

His passion for service drew him to the medical career; and soon he gravitated to where he thought that his service was most needed. Malaya claimed him. He had earlier been editing a health journal and wrote extensively on health problems. He discovered that people needed right knowledge most of all; dissemination of that knowledge he espoused as his own mission.

It was divine dispensation and the blessing of God upon mankind that the doctor of body and mind renounced his career and took to a life of renunciation to qualify for ministering to the soul of man. He settled down at Rishikesh in 1924, practised intense austerities and shone as a great Yogi, saint, sage and Jivanmukta.

In 1932 Swami Sivananda started the Sivanandashram. In 1936 was born The Divine Life Society. In 1948 the Yoga-Vedanta Forest Academy was organised. Dissemination of spiritual knowledge and training of people in Yoga and Vedanta were their aim and object. In 1950 Swamiji undertook a lightning tour of India and Ceylon. In 1953 Swamiji convened a 'World Parliament of Religions'. Swamiji is the author of over 300 volumes and has disciples all over the world, belonging to all nationalities, religions and creeds. To read Swamiji's works is to drink at the Fountain of Wisdom Supreme. On 14th July, 1963 Swamiji entered Mahasamadhi.

PREFACE

The present edition of this immensely useful work 'Japa Yoga' by His Holiness Swami Sivanandaji Maharaj is brought out in response to several requests that we have received from devotees everywhere. We need not emphasise the importance of this work as its subject-matter forms the foundation of spiritual Sadhana. *Yajnanam Japayajnosmi*—I am the sacrifice of Japa among all sacrifices, says the Lord in the Gita. It is the continuous recitation of the Divine Name that forms the first rung in the ladder of Yoga, as also the undercurrent that flows beneath the different processes of Yoga.

The subject of this book is such that it will become a *vade mecum* for all seekers on the path. We cannot think of another book on the subject so handy and exhaustive to be placed in the hands of Sadhakas. The chapters are methodically arranged to suit the conveniences of readers and provide a graduated series of lessons on this significant aspect of Bhakti Yoga.

We have no doubt that this incomparable treatise will be received by one and all with the rich approbation and the commendation that it deserves. May the Grace of Almighty be upon us all.

—The Divine Life Society

सद्गुरुस्तोत्रम्

ॐ ब्रह्मानन्दं परमसुखदं केवलं ज्ञानमूर्तिं

द्वन्द्वातीतं गगनसदृशं तत्त्वमस्यादिलक्ष्यम्।

एकं नित्यं विमलमचलं सर्वधीसाक्षिभूतं

भावातीतं त्रिगुणरहितं सद्गुरुं तं नमामि ॥१॥

1. I prostrate myself before that Sat-Guru, the Brahman, who is Bliss, who is the giver of Supreme happiness, who is the Absolute, who is the Form of Knowledge, who is beyond the pairs of opposites, who is (vast) like ether, who is attainable through assertions like "Tat Tvam Asi", who is one, eternal, pure and changeless, who is the witness of all the states of the mind, who transcends modifications, who is devoid of the three modes (of Prakriti).

चैतन्यं शाश्वतं शान्तं व्योमातीतं निरञ्जनम्।

नादबिन्दुकलातीतं तस्मै श्रीगुरवे नमः ॥२॥

2. Prostrations to that Sri-Guru, who is Consciousness, eternal, peaceful, beyond ether, spotless and beyond Nada, Bindu and Kala.

गुरुर्ब्रह्मा गुरुर्विष्णुर्गुरुर्देवो महेश्वरः।

गुरुः साक्षात् परं ब्रह्म तस्मै श्रीगुरवे नमः ॥३॥

3. Prostration to that Sri-Guru, who is himself the gods Brahma, Vishnu and Mahesvara, and who is verily the supreme Absolute itself.

ॐ नमः शिवाय गुरवे सच्चिदानन्दमूर्तये।

निष्प्रपञ्चाय शान्ताय निरालम्बाय तेजसे ॥४॥

4. Om! Prostration to the Guru, who, is Siva (bliss and auspiciousness), who is the embodiment of Existence-Knowledge-Bliss, who is free from world-consciousness, who is peaceful, without (any other) support, and self-effulgent.

DHYANA SLOKAS

ॐकारस्तोत्रम्

ॐकारं निगमैकवेद्यमनिशं वेदान्ततत्त्वास्पदं
चोत्पत्तिस्थितिनाशहेतुममलं विश्वस्य विश्वात्मकम्।
विश्वत्राणपरायणं श्रुतिशतैः संप्रोच्यमानं विभुं
सत्यज्ञानमनन्तमूर्तिममलं शुद्धात्मकं तं भजे॥

I always contemplate upon the ever-pure, all-pervading Omkara (Pranava), which can be known only through the Vedas, which is the essence and the support of the Vedanta, which is taintless, which is the cause of the creation, preservation and destruction of the universe, which includes the whole universe within itself, which is the saviour of the universe, which is proclaimed by countless Srutis, and which is the pure truth, knowledge and infinity in one.

गणपतिस्तोत्रम्

गजाननं भूतगणादिसेवितं कपित्थजम्बूफलसारभक्षणम्।
उमासुतं शोकविनाशकारणं नमामि विघ्नेश्वरपादपङ्कजम्॥

I prostrate myself before the lotus-feet of Vighnesvara, the son of Uma, the cause of the destruction of sorrow, who is served by the host of Bhuta-Ganas, etc., who has the face of an elephant, who partakes of the essence of Kapittha and Jambu fruits.

विष्णुस्तोत्रम्

शान्ताकारं भुजगशयनं पद्मनाभं सुरेशं
विश्वाधारं गगनसदृशं मेघवर्णं शुभांङ्गम्।
लक्ष्मीकान्तं कमलनयनं योगिभिर्ध्यानगम्यं
वन्दे विष्णुं भवभयहरं सर्वलोकैकनाथम्॥

I adore Vishnu, the embodiment of Peace, who sleeps on the serpent, whose navel is the lotus (of the universe), who is the Lord of gods, who is the support of the universe, who is of the form of (the omnipresent) ether, whose colour resembles that of clouds, whose body is auspicious, who is the Lord of Lakshmi, whose eyes are like lotuses, who is attainable by Yogis through meditation, who is the destroyer of the fear of birth and death, and who is the One Lord of all the worlds.

शिवस्तोत्रम्

शान्तं पद्मासनस्थं शशधरमकुटं पञ्चवक्त्रं त्रिनेत्रं
शूलं वज्रं च खड्गं परशुमभयदं दक्षभागे वहन्तम्।
नागं पाशं च घण्टां डमरुकसहितं साङ्कुशं वामभागे
नानालङ्कारदीप्तं स्फटिकमणिनिभं पार्वतीशं नमामि ।।

I prostrate myself, before the Lord of Parvati, who is peaceful, who is seated in the Lotus-pose, whose crown is adorned with moon, who has five faces, who has three eyes, who holds the trident, bolt, sword and the fearlessness-giving axe on the right side, who holds the serpent, noose, bell, Damaru and spear on the left side, who shines with various ornaments, and who is luminous like the crystal-jewel.

देवीस्तोत्रम्

विद्युद्दामसमप्रभां मृगपतिस्कन्धस्थितां भीषणाम्
कन्याभिः करवालखेटविलसद्धस्ताभिरासेविताम्।
हस्तैश्चक्रदरालिखेटविशिखांश्चापं गुणं तर्जनीम्
बिभ्राणामनलात्मिकां शशिधरां दुर्गां त्रिनेत्रां भजे ।।

I worship the three-eyed Durga, whose lustre is like that of a streak of lightning, who is seated on the lord of animals (lion), who is the dreadful, who is served by maidens holding weapons and clubs in their hands, who holds with her hands discus, conch, liquor, clubs, arrows, bow with its string drawn in with the fingers, who is blazing like fire and who wears the moon (on the crown).

लक्ष्मीस्तोत्रम्

लक्ष्मीं क्षीरसमुद्रराजतनयां श्रीरङ्गधामेश्वरीं
दासीभूतसमस्तदेववनितां लोकैकदीपाङ्कुराम्।
श्रीमन्मन्दकटाक्षलब्धविभवब्रह्मेन्द्रगङ्गाधरां
त्वां त्रैलोक्यकुटुम्बिनीं सरसिजां वन्दे मुकुन्दप्रियाम्॥

I worship that Lakshmi, the daughter of the king of the milk-ocean, the queen of the abode of Lord Vishnu, whose servants are the wives of all the gods, who is the one light and the sprout of the universe, through a side glance of whose benign grace Brahma, Indra and Siva have attained their high positions, who is the mother of the three worlds, who is called Kamala, and who is the consort of Bhagavan Vishnu.

सरस्वतीस्तोत्रम्

या कुन्देन्दुतुषारहारधवला या शुभ्रावस्त्रावृता
या वीणावरदण्ड मण्डितकरा या श्वेतपद्मासना।
या ब्रह्माच्युतशङ्करप्रभृतिभिर्देवैस्सदा पूजिता
सा मां पातु सरस्वती भगवती निःशेषजाड्यापहा॥

May that goddess Sarasvati, who wears a garland white like the Kunda-flower or the moon or the snow, who is adorned with pure white clothes, whose hands are ornamented with the Vina and the gesture of blessings, who is seated on a white lotus, who is always worshipped by Brahma, Vishnu, Siva and other gods, who is the remover of all inertness and laziness protect me.

रामस्तोत्रम्

ध्यायेदाजानुबाहुं धृतशरधनुषं बद्धपद्मासनस्थं
पीतं वासो वसानं नवकमलदलस्पर्धिनेत्रं प्रसन्नम्।
वामाङ्कारूढसीतामुखकमलमिलल्लोचनं नीरदाभं
नानालङ्कारदीप्तं दधतमुरुजटामण्डलं रामचन्द्रम्॥

One should meditate upon Sri Ramachandra, with hands reaching the knees, holding the bow and the arrows, seated in the locked-up lotus-posture, wearing a yellow cloth, with eyes vying with the newly blossomed lotus-petals, with a pleasant gait, with his eyes mixing with the lotus-face of Sita seated on his left thigh, who is blue like the clouds, who is shining with various kinds of ornaments, and who has a big circle of Jata on the head.

कृष्णस्तोत्रम्

वंशीविभूषितकरान्नवनीरदाभात्
पीताम्बरादरुणबिम्बफलाधरोष्ठात्।
पूर्णेन्दुसुन्दरमुखादरविन्दनेत्रात्
कृष्णात्परं किमपि तत्त्वमहं न जाने॥

I know not any other reality than the lotus-eyed Krishna, with hands adorned with the flute, looking like a newly laden cloud in lustre, wearing a yellow silk garment, with his lips like a ruddy Bimba-fruit, and with his face beautiful like the full-moon.

सुब्रह्मण्यस्तोत्रम्

षडाननं कुङ्कुमरक्तवर्णं
महामतिं दिव्यमयूरवाहनम्
रुद्रस्य सूनुं सुरसैन्यनाथं
गुहं सदाऽहं शरणं प्रपद्ये॥

I always take refuge in Guha of six faces, who is of deep red colour like Kumkuma, who is possessed of great knowledge, who has the divine peacock to ride on, who is the son of Rudra, and who is the leader of the army of gods.

भगवत्स्तोत्रम्

यं ब्रह्मावरुणेन्द्ररुद्रमरुतः स्तुन्वन्ति दिव्यैः स्तवै-
र्वेदैः साङ्गपदक्रमोपनिषदैर्गायन्ति यं सामगाः।

ध्यानावस्थिततद्गतेन मनसा पश्यन्ति यं योगिनो
यस्यान्तं न विदुः सुरासुरगणा देवाय तस्मै नमः ॥

Salutations to that God whom Brahma, Varuna, Indra, Rudra, and the Maruts praise with divine hymns, whom the Sama-chanters sing by Vedas with their Angas and in the Pada and Krama methods and by the Upanishads, whom Yogis see with their minds absorbed in Him through meditation, and whose end the hosts of Devas and Asuras know not.

PRAYERS TO THE LORD

I

O Adorable Lord of Compassion! Salutations unto Thee. Give me inner spiritual strength to resist temptation and melt in Thee this ego which is harder than granite or diamond. Let me always be Thy chosen playmate in the wonderful game You play in all the worlds. Let me understand Thy mysterious Lila or sporting. Let me be a perennial channel of Thy sweet love to all Thy children. Utilise my body, the senses and the mind for Thy unhampered play. O hidden Love! O undecaying beauty! Let my soul rest peacefully in Thee for ever and ever.

O Light of lights! O shining One! I live for Thee. I behold Thee in the smiles of children, in the tears of the afflicted, in my thoughts, emotions, sentiments, in the morning dew of the Himalayan landscape and in the rays of the sun. My room is filled with Thy sweet Presence. I eat Thy benign grace in my daily food. I taste Thy radiant love in my daily drink. Thou art the ocean of love and compassion. Let my love for Thee become a roaring flame. Withdraw from me whatever evil there is. Fill my heart with purity, goodness, love and sublime virtues. Make me Immortal.

O Lord! Reveal unto me Thy enchanting Form. Make me feel Thy living Presence. Fill my heart with love. Let me merge myself in Thee. Let me walk in the path of righteousness. Cleanse my mind of all evil thoughts. Help me to concentrate my mind on Thy lotus-feet. Embrace me and make me pure. Teach me to be still and enjoy Thy magnificent Vision. Illumine my mind with the light of true Knowledge. Make my stony heart melt and flow towards Thee.

II

Thou art, O Lord, the creator of this universe. Thou art the protector of this world. Thou art in the grass and in the rose. Thou art in the sun and the stars. Salutations unto Thee. O Bestower of joy and bliss!

Sweet Lord! Let me be free from the clutches of death. Let me be able to look upon all beings with equal vision. Let me be free from impurity and sin. Give me strength to control the mind. Give me strength to serve Thee and the humanity untiringly. Make me Thy fit instrument for Thy work. Make me pure and strong.

I bow to Thee, O Indweller of all hearts! O Secret of secrets! Remove my weaknesses, defects and evil thoughts. Make me pure, so that I may be able to receive Thy grace and blessings. O Lord! Thou art the thread-soul that connects all beings. Thou pervadest all, permeatest and interpenetratest all things of this Universe.

Thou art the Light Divine. Thou art the Dispeller of ignorance. Thou art the All-merciful Lord. Give me a life without disease. Let me remember Thee always. Let me develop all the sublime virtues.

Thou art self-luminous. Thou art my Father, Mother, Brother, Friend, Relative and Guide. Let me realise the Truth. Let me be free from greed, lust, egoism, jealousy and hatred. Prepare me as Thy sweet messenger on this earth, so that I may radiate joy; peace and bliss to the whole world. Let me utilise my body, mind and senses in Thy service and in the service of Thy creatures. Breathe into me Thy breath of Immortality. Let me recognise the Universal Brotherhood of Man. Let me love all as my own Self. Salutations unto Thee! O Lord of Compassion!

III

O Adorable Lord of Compassion! Salutations unto Thee! Thou art Infinite Beauty, Joy, Bliss and Peace! Thou art Perfect, Independent and ever Free! Give me the spirit of sacrifice, strength and indomitable will to serve humanity! Vouchsafe to me Thy grace and mercy!

O Almighty! Thou art my Redeemer and Saviour. Free me from the bondage of this body and round of births and deaths. Make me drink the nectar of Immortality!

O Supreme Being! Fill my heart with unflinching devotion unto Thee. Let the flame of devotion to Thee grow brighter every day!

O Infinity! O Eternity! O Immortality! Free me from all sorrows, dependence, delusion, weakness and defects! Grant me equal vision, balanced mind, divine virtues, such as courage, tolerance, forbearance, humility, mercy, purity, cosmic love, etc.

O Omnipotent Lord! Strengthen my resolve to stick to the spiritual path and to do my daily spiritual routine vigorously and regularly. Forgive my sins. Free me from the obstacles in the path and from all temptations. Give me inner strength to resist temptations!

O Indwelling Presence! Thou art my sole prop, support, refuge and solace! Thou art the Life of my life. Thou art the Soul of my soul. Thou art Transcendental Bliss, Peace and Joy. Thou art the one homogeneous essence. Let me be established in Nonviolence, Truthfulness, Devotion and Purity. Teach me to be steadfast in my devotion unto Thee. Give me Light and Wisdom.

O Supreme Love! Salutations unto Thee! Thou art the Indweller of my heart. Give me the inner third eye of intuition or wisdom. May Self-realisation be my inexhaustible spiritual wealth, dispassion my crown, virtuous deeds my asset in the divine bank, and renunciation the jewel of my heart! Crores of prostrations unto Thee, O Lord, I am Thine. Save me, protect me, guide me and enlighten me. Make me pure, perfect and free! Through Thy grace may all attain health, long life, prosperity and Self-realisation!

UNIVERSAL PRAYER

O Adorable Lord of Mercy and Love!
Salutations and prostrations unto Thee.
Thou art Omnipresent, Omnipotent and Omniscient;
Thou art Satchidananda.
Thou art the Indweller of all beings.

Grant us an understanding heart,
Equal vision, balanced mind,
Faith, devotion and wisdom.
Grant us inner spiritual strength
To resist temptations and to control the mind.
Free us from egoism, lust, greed, hatred,
anger and jealousy.
Fill our hearts with divine virtues.

Let us behold Thee in all these names and forms.
Let us serve Thee in all these names and forms.
Let us ever remember Thee.
Let us ever sing Thy Glories.
Let Thy Name be ever on our lips.
Let us abide in Thee for ever and ever.

विश्वप्रार्थना

(Sanskrit)

हे वन्दनीय प्रेमाधार हे कृपानिधे
नमोऽस्तु ते साष्टाङ्गं नमोऽस्तु ते।
भगवान् सर्वव्यापी सर्वशक्तिमान् सर्वज्ञः
भगवान् सच्चिदानन्दः सर्वान्तर्यामी।
विवेकं च समदर्शनं च मनसस्समत्वं च

अथ श्रद्धां च भक्तिं च ज्ञानं च देहि नः।
आध्यात्मिकान्तःशक्तिमपि देहि नः
येनोपायेन मायां विहाय मनो वशं कुर्महे।
कामक्रोधलोभाहंकारेभ्यो मोचयास्मान्
दैवीसंपद्भिरस्माकं हृदयानि पूरय।

सर्वनामरूपेषु त्वां ईक्षामहे
तेषु नामरूपेषु त्वां ईक्षामहे
तेषु नामरूपेषु त्वां सेवामहे
सर्वदा त्वामेव स्मरामः।
सर्वदा तव महिम्नां गानं करवामहै।
अस्माकं ओष्ठेषु तव नामैव भूयात्।
सर्वदा भवत्प्राणा एव भूयास्म।

विश्व-प्रार्थना

(Hindi)

हे स्नेह और करुणा के आराध्य देव!
तुम्हें नमस्कार है, नमस्कार है।
तुम सर्वव्यापक, सर्वशक्तिमान् और सर्वज्ञ हो।
तुम सच्चिदानन्दघन हो।
तुम सबके अन्तर्वासी हो।

हमें उदारता, समदर्शिता और मन का समत्व प्रदान करो।
श्रद्धा, भक्ति और प्रज्ञा से कृतार्थ करो।
हमें आध्यात्मिक अन्त:शक्ति का वर दो,
जिससे हम वासनाओं का दमन कर मनोजय को प्राप्त हों।
हम अहंकार, काम, लोभ, घृणा, क्रोध और द्वेष से रहित हों।
हमारा हृदय दिव्य गुणों से परिपूरित करो।

हम सब नाम-रूपों में तुम्हारा दर्शन करें।
तुम्हारी अर्चना के ही रूप में इन नाम-रूपों की सेवा करें।
सदा तुम्हारा ही स्मरण करें।
सदा तुम्हारी ही महिमा का गान करें।
तुम्हारा ही कलिकल्मषहारी नाम हमारे अधर-पुट पर हो।
सदा हम तुममें ही निवास करें।

—स्वामी शिवानन्द

॥ महामृत्युञ्जयमन्त्रः ॥

MAHA-MRITYUNJAYA MANTRA

ॐ त्र्यंबकं यजामहे सुगन्धिं पुष्टिवर्धनम् ।
उर्वारुकमिव बन्धनान्मृत्योर्मुक्षीय माऽमृतात् ॥

Om Tryambakam yajamahe
Sugandhim pushtivardhanam;
Urvaarukamiva bandhanaan-
Mrityormuksheeya maamritaat.

"We worship the three-eyed One (Lord Siva) who is fragrant and who nourishes all beings; may He liberate me from death, for the sake of Immortality, even as the cucumber is severed from its bondage (of the creeper)."

1. This Maha-Mrityunjaya Mantra is a life-giving Mantra. In these days, when life is very complex, accidents are an everyday affair; this Mantra wards off deaths by snake-bites, lightning, motor-accidents, fire-accidents, cycle-accidents, water-accidents, air-accidents and accidents of all descriptions. Besides, it has a great curative effect. Again, diseases pronounced incurable by doctors are cured by this Mantra, when chanted with sincerity, faith and devotion. It is a weapon against all diseases. It is a Mantra to conquer death.

2. It is also a Moksha-Mantra. It is Lord Siva's Mantra. It bestows health (Arogya), long life (Deergha-Ayus), peace (Santi), wealth (Aisvarya), prosperity (Pushti), satisfaction (Tushti) and Immortality (Moksha).

3. On your birthday, repeat this Mantra one lakh times, or at least 50,000 times, perform Havan and feed Sadhus, the poor and the sick. This will bestow on you health, long life, peace, prosperity and Moksha.

PRAYER TO THE SUN

ॐ सूर्यं सुन्दरलोकनाथममृतं वेदान्तसारं शिवं
ज्ञानं ब्रह्ममयं सुरेशममलं लोकैकचित्तं स्वयम्।
इन्द्रादित्यनराधिपं सुरगुरुं त्रैलोक्यचूडामणिं
ब्रह्माविष्णुशिवस्वरूपहृदयं वन्दे सदा भास्करम्।।

"Om Suryam sundaralokanathamamritam
vedantasaram sivam,
Jnanam brahmamayam suresamamalam
lokaikachittam svayam;
Indradityanaradhipam suragurum trailokyachudamanim,
Brahmavishnusiva svarupa hridayam vande
sada bhaskaram."

I always adore Surya, the sun, the beautiful Lord of the world, the immortal, the quintessence of the Vedanta, the auspicious, the absolute knowledge, of the form of Brahman, the Lord of the gods, ever-pure, the one true consciousness of the world himself, the Lord of Indra, the gods and men, the preceptor of the gods, the crest-jewel of the three worlds, the very heart of the forms of Brahma, Vishnu and Siva, the giver of light.

ॐ हिरणमयेन पात्रेण सत्यस्यापिहितं मुखम्।
तत्त्वं पूषन्नपावृणु सत्यधर्माय दृष्टये।।
पूषन्नेकर्षे यम सूर्य प्राजापत्य व्यूह रश्मीन् समूह।
तेजो यत्ते रूपम कल्याणतमं तत्ते पश्यामि
योऽसावसौ पुरुषः सोऽहमस्मि।।

Om Hiranmayena patrena satyasyapihitam mukham,

Tattvam pushan apavrinu satyadharmaya drishtaye.

Pushan ekarshe yama surya prajapatya
vyuha rasmin samuha,

Tejo yatte rupam kalyanatamam tatte pasyami
yosavasau purushah sohamasmi.

"The face of Truth is covered by a golden vessel. Remove Thou, O sun, that covering, for the law of Truth to behold (It)."

"O Pushan (sun, nourisher), the only Seer (sole traveller of the heavens), controller of all (Yama), Surya, son of Prajapati; disperse Thy rays and gather up Thy burning light; I behold Thy glorious resplendent form; I am He, the Purusha within Thee."

1. ॐ मित्राय नमः (*Om Mitraya Namah*)
   Prostration to Him who is affectionate to all.
2. ॐ रवये नमः (*Om Ravaye Namah*)
   Prostration to Him who is the cause for change.
3. ॐ सूर्याय नमः (*Om Suryaya Namah*)
   Prostration to Him who induces activity.
4. ॐ भानवे नमः (*Om Bhanave Namah*)
   Prostration to Him who diffuses Light.
5. ॐ खगाय नमः (*Om Khagaya Namah*)
   Prostration to Him who moves in the sky.
6. ॐ पूष्णे नमः (*Om Pushne Namah*)
   Prostration to Him who nourishes all.
7. ॐ हिरण्यगर्भाय नमः (*Om Hiranyagarbhaya Namah)*
   Prostration to Him who contains everything.
8. ॐ मरीचये नमः (*Om Marichaye Namah*)
   Prostration to him who possesses rays.
9. ॐ आदित्याय नमः (*Om Adityaya Namah*)
   Prostration to Him who is God of gods.
10. ॐ सवित्रे नमः (*Om Savitre Namah*)
    Prostration to Him who produces everything.
11. ॐ अर्काय नमः (*Om Arkaya Namah*)
    Prostration to Him who is fit to be worshipped.
12. ॐ भास्कराय नमः (*Om Bhaskaraya Namah*)
    Prostration to Him who is the cause of lustre.

In the words of Yajurveda:

"O Sun! O Sun of suns! Thou art All-energy, give me energy; Thou art All-strength, give me strength; Thou art All-powerful, give me power."

Repeat the above Mantras and Names of the Sun at sunrise. He who repeats these before sunrise, early in the morning, will possess wonderful health, vigour and vitality. He will be free from every kind of disease of the eye. He will have wonderful eye-sight. Pray to the sun in the early morning, before sunrise: "O Lord, Suryanarayana, the eye of the world, the eye of the Virat-Purusha; give me health, strength, vigour and vitality." Offer Arghya to the sun during the three Sandhyas (morning, noon and evening). Offer prostrations to the sun, with these Mantras and Names.

PRAYER TO HARI

सर्वस्मिन् सर्वभूतस्त्वं सर्वः सर्वस्वरूपधृक्।
सर्वं त्वत्तस्ततश्च त्वमेवं सर्वात्मने नमः॥

सर्वात्मकोऽसि सर्वेश सर्वभूतस्थितो यतः।
कथयामि ततः किं ते सर्वं वेत्सि हृदि स्थितम्॥

Thou abidest in all. Thou hast become all beings. Thou art the all. Thou assumest all forms; all are from Thee; hence Thou art the all, the Soul of all. Glory unto Thee, the Self of all beings.

As Thou art the Soul of all, the Lord of all, and present in all beings, what shall I speak unto Thee? Thou knowest everything in (my) mind (being seated in the hearts of all beings).

ॐ

Dear brothers,

Japa is the repetition of any mantra or name of the Lord. In this iron age Japa is the easiest and surest way for God-realisation.

Repeat 200 malas of Japa daily. Mala or rosary is a whip to goad the mind towards God. Wear a mala in your neck. It is the most precious jewel or ornament as it reminds you of God.

Practice of Japa removes the impurities of the mind, destroys sins and brings the devotee face to face with God. Japa must become habitual. Be regular in your Japa.

Sivananda

ॐ

Friends,

The glory of the name of God cannot be established through reasoning. It can certainly be experienced through faith, devotion and constant repetition. Have reverence and faith for the name. Do not argue.

Every name is filled with countless powers. Just as fire has the natural property of burning things, so also the name of God has the power of burning the sins and desires.

O Man! Take refuge in the name and cross this formidable ocean of birth and death. Name and Nami are inseparable. Glory to the Lord. Glory to His name. Hari OM. Sri Ram.

Sivananda

INTRODUCTION

I

In this Kali Yuga (iron age) Japa alone is the easy way to the realisation of God. The famous author of a commentary on the Gita and of the Advaita Siddhi, Swami Madhusudana Saraswati, had direct Darsan of Lord Krishna through Japa of the Mantra of Lord Krishna. The reputed Swami Vidyaranya, the author of the Panchadasi had direct Darsan of Mother Gayatri through Japa of Gayatri Mantra.

At the present moment many educated persons and college-students have lost faith in the power of Mantra, owing to the morbid influence of the study of science. They have entirely given up Japa. It is highly deplorable indeed. When the blood is warm they become hot-headed, proud and atheistic. Their brains and minds need a thorough overhauling and drastic flushing.

Life is short. Time is fleeting. The world is full of miseries. Cut the knot of Avidya, and drink the Nirvanic Bliss. That day on which you do not perform any Japa is simply wasted. Those who simply eat, drink and sleep and do not practise any Japa are horizontal beings only.

A Mantra, in the Hindu religion, has a Rishi who gave it to the world; a metre which governs the inflection of the voice; and a Devata or a supernatural being, higher or lower, as its informing power. The Bija, seed, is a significant word, or series of words, which gives it a special power. Sometimes this word is a sound which harmonises with the key-note of the individual using it and varies it with individuals; sometimes this word expresses the essence of the Mantra, and the result of the Mantra is the flower springing from this seed. The Sakti is the energy of the form of the Mantra, i.e., the vibration-forms set up by its sounds. These carry the man to the Devata that is worshipped. The Kilaka, the pillar, is that which supports and makes strong the Mantra, or the pin which fastens the Mantra together; this is the ceasing of sorrow, by the freeing of oneself from imperfections.

Do not bother yourself about Matra, Para and Pasyanti, etc. Do Japa of your Ishta Mantra mentally with its meaning and right Bhava. You will realise the spiritual benefits. Why do you waste your time counting the pebbles on the bank? Take a dip immediately in the Ganges and enjoy the bath. Become wise.

All Mantras have equal potency or power. It is incorrect to say that Om Namo Narayanaya is superior to Om Namah Sivaya or Radhesyam or Sri Ram, and so on. You can attain God-realisation by doing Japa of any Mantra. Valmiki attained God-consciousness by repeating even Mara-Mara. Some people think that Om or Soham is superior to Om Namo Narayanaya, or vice versa. This also is wrong. The state gained by doing Japa of Om or Soham can be attained by doing Japa of Sri Ram or Radhesyam also.

You should not doubt the teachings of the scriptures. Flickering faith will lead to downfall. A man of weak will, who has no faith in Japa, cannot expect to have progress in the spiritual path. If he says, "I am practising 'who am I' enquiry"—this is all wild imagination. Few are fit for "who am I" enquiry.

You must have the Bhava that Atman, Isvara, Devata, Mantra are one. With this Bhava you will have to repeat your Guru Mantra or Ishta Mantra. Then alone you will have Mantra Siddhi or God-realisation quickly.

The Japa of a Mantra can bring to the practitioner realisation of his highest goal though he may not possess knowledge of the meaning of the Mantra. Such a mechanical Japa may take a little more time in realisation than when it is practised with a knowledge of the meaning. There is an indescribable power or Achintya Sakti in the Mantras. If you repeat the Mantra with concentration on its meaning, you will attain God-consciousness quickly.

Form a strong habit of repeating the Name of the Lord. Then only it will be easy for you to remember Him at the time of death.

To define God is to deny God. You can give the definition of a finite object. How can you define limitless or the Infinite Being who is the source and ultimate cause for everything? If you define God you are limiting the limitless one, you are confining

Him with concepts of mind. God is beyond the reach of the gross mind, but He can be realised through Japa and meditation with a pure, subtle and one-pointed mind.

II

Manasika Puja (mental worship) is more powerful than external Puja with flowers, etc. Arjuna thought that Bhima was not doing any kind of worship. He was proud of his external worship of Lord Siva. He offered plenty of Bael leaves. But Bhima offered to the Lord mentally the Bael leaves of all the Bael trees of the whole world. He was doing Manasika Puja of Lord Siva. The attendants of Lord Siva were not able to remove from the head of Lord Siva the Bael leaves offered by Bhima. Arjuna once saw a large band of people carrying baskets of Bael leaves. He thought within himself that the leaves must be those offered by him to Lord Siva and questioned them thus: "Brothers, from where do you carry these Bael leaves?" They replied: "O Arjuna, these leaves are offered to our Lord Siva by Bhima through Manasika Puja." Arjuna was struck with wonder. He came to know that Manasika Puja was more powerful than external worship and that Bhima was a better devotee than he.

Manasika Puja can be done by advanced students. Beginners should certainly do worship with flowers, sandal paste, incense, etc. You will have more concentration when you do Manasika Puja. Mentally enthrone the Lord in Simhasana set with diamonds, pearls, emeralds, etc. Offer Him a seat. Apply sandal paste to His forehead and body. Offer Arghya, Madhuparka and various sorts of flowers, clothes, etc. Burn incense. Wave lights. Burn camphor. Offer various kinds of fruits, sweetmeats and Maha Naivedya. Offer to the Lord the fruits of the whole world. Do not be miserly even in Manasika Puja. In Manasika Puja one man offered only one stale plantain fruit and a handful of gram. A miserable miserly man! Even in Manasika Puja he cannot be very generous and liberal! This world abounds with such deplorable misers! In the end mentally repeat: "*Kayena vacha manasendriyairva buddhyatmana va prakritessvabhavat, karomi yadyat sakalam parasmai narayanayeti samarpayami*—whatever action I do by the body, by the speech, by the mind, by the senses, by the intellect or by my own nature, I offer all of them to the supreme Lord

Narayana." Also say in the end, "*Om Tat Sat Brahmarpanamastu.*" This will purify your heart and remove the taint of expectation of reward.

III

Without love man's life is empty. Without love man lives in vain. Love is vital. It is all-pervading. Love is a greater power. Love is the sap of life. Give love. Cultivate this love through service, Japa, Satsanga and meditation.

God is always with you. He will protect and deliver you. Take refuge in Him. His blessings overflow into your life and transform your mind and body. Develop your consciousness of spiritual things. Make a special effort daily to exercise control over your thoughts, words and actions. Feel His presence in your room. Pray and meditate daily.

Prayer elevates the mind. It fills the mind with purity. It is associated with praise of God. It keeps the mind in tune with God. Prayer can reach a realm where reason does not dare to enter. Prayer can move mountains. It can work miracles. It frees the devotee from the fear of death. It brings him nearer to God and makes him feel the divine consciousness and his essential, immortal and blissful nature.

Surrender everything to Him. Place your ego at His feet and be at ease. He will take complete charge of you. Let Him mould you in any way He likes. Let Him do exactly as He wills. He will remove all defects and weaknesses. He will play beautifully on this body-flute. Hear this marvellous music of His flute, the mysterious music of the Soul, and rejoice.

Make your offerings to the Lord with the same mental attitude as that of Bhilini Sabari. Call the Lord with the same Bhava of Draupadi or with the Bhava which Gajendra had when he called Lord Hari. You will surely meet your Beloved. Develop this Bhava. You will have the Darsan of the Lord immediately.

Feel His Presence everywhere. Strive ceaselessly to fix your mind on the Lord. Try to constantly behold your Beloved in all these forms. Silently repeat His Names. Sometimes sing His Names. Silently do Kirtan. Melt the mind in Him. Rejoice in silence in Him.

If you get up at Brahmamuhurta, at 4 a.m., you will have a clear mind. There is a spiritual influence and mysterious silence in the early morning hours. All saints and Yogis practise meditation at this period and send their spiritual vibrations to the whole world. You will be highly benefited by their vibrations if you start your prayer, Japa and meditation at this period. You need not exert much. The meditative state of mind will come by itself.

Gaze at the picture of the Lord, your Ishta-Devata, for a few minutes, and close your eyes. Then try to visualise the picture mentally. You will have a well-defined or clear-cut picture of the Lord. When it fades, open your eyes and gaze. Repeat the process 5 or 6 times. You will be able to visualise clearly your Ishta-Devata or tutelary deity mentally, after some months' practice.

If you find it difficult to visualise the whole picture, try to visualise any part of the picture. Try to produce at least a hazy picture. By repeated practice the hazy picture will assume a well-defined, clear-cut form. If you find this to be difficult, fix the mind on the effulgent light in the heart and take this as the form of the Lord or your Ishta.

The thoughts you create in your mind and the images you form in your daily life help you in making what you are or what you would become. If you constantly think of Lord Krishna, you will become identical with the Lord. You will abide in Him for ever. You will become one with the Deity you meditate upon.

In Bhava-Samadhi the mind of the devotee is highly elevated through pure emotion and devotion. He forgets the body and the world. His mind is wholly absorbed in the Lord.

Contentment, unruffled state of the mind, cheerfulness, patience, decrease in excretions, sweet voice, eagerness and steadiness in the practice of meditation, disgust for worldly prosperity and success and company, desire to remain alone in a quiet room or in seclusion, desire for association with Sadhus and Sannyasins, Ekagrata or one-pointedness of mind, are some of the signs that indicate that you are growing in purity, that you are progressing in the spiritual path.

When you enter the silence through deep meditation the world outside and all your troubles will drop away. You will enjoy supreme peace. In the silence is the Supreme Light of lights. In the silence is undecaying bliss. In this silence is real strength and perennial joy.

Shut out the doors of the senses. Still the thoughts, emotions and feelings. Sit motionless and calm in the early morning hours. Ignore the visions and coloured lights. Have a receptive attitude. Go alone with God. Commune with Him. Enjoy the abiding peace in silence.

In the Srimad Bhagavata the Lord Sri Krishna says to Uddhava, "I am not so easily attainable by Yoga, Sankhya or discrimination, Dharma, study of the Vedas, Tapas, renunciation, liberal gifts, charitable acts, rites such as Agnihotra, fasts, vows, secret Mantras, resort to pilgrimages, Yamas, Niyamas (moral rules), as by Satsanga (company of Sadhus or the wise) which puts an end to all attachments. It is only by association with the wise and the righteous, that many who were of Rajasic or Tamasic nature—such as Vritra, son of the sage Tvashtri; Prahlada, the Daityas, the Asuras and the Rakshasas, Gandharvas, Apsaras, Nagas, Siddhas, Charanas, Guhyakas and Vidyadharas, many beasts and birds, and among mankind Vaisyas, Sudras, women and outcastes who are of the lowest birth, have attained Me. Vrishaparva, Bali, Bana, Maya, Vibhishana, Sugriva, Hanuman; Jambavan, the bear; Gajendra, the elephant; Jatayu, the vulture; Tuladhara, the merchant; Dharmavyadha, the fowler; Kubja, the hunch-backed perfume-seller; the Gopis in Vraja, the wives of the Brahmanas engaged in sacrifices in Brindavana, and others—all these did not study the Vedas, did not sit at the feet of great men of learning for the sake of knowledge. They did not observe any vows or fasts. They did not perform Tapas but they attained Me through association with saints and Sadhus. Through love alone, developed through the company of saints, the Gopis and even the cows, trees, beasts, serpents and others of dull-witted nature, became perfected and easily attained Me whom one does not attain by making great endeavours through Yoga or Sankhya, charity, vows, Tapas, sacrifices, teaching and study of the Vedas or renunciation.

Satsanga or association with the sages removes the darkness of the heart. It is a safe boat to cross the ocean of Samsara. Satsanga elevates the mind and fills it with Sattva or purity. It eradicates vicious thoughts and impressions in the heart. It leads one to the right path and causes the Sun of Wisdom to shine upon one's mind.

You may do Japa of 'Om Namah Sivaya' Mantra, if you are a votary of Lord Siva, or 'Om Namo Narayanaya' if you are a devotee of Lord Vishnu. These are very powerful Mantras. None can explain the benefits of Japa, Sadhana and Satsanga. Japa is the rod in the hands of the blind Sadhakas to plod on the road to realisation. Japa is the philosopher's stone or divine elixir that makes one God-like. Through Japa alone one can realise God in this life.

This book will throw much light on the important subject of Mantra Yoga and the method of attaining perfection through Japa. The First Chapter gives the definition of Japa. The Second Chapter deals with the glory and importance of the Name of God. Different kinds of Mantras are given in the Third Chapter. The Fourth Chapter contains many practical and useful instructions on Sadhana. The Fifth Chapter gives a short sketch of the lives of some of the saints who realised God through Japa.

May God give you inner strength to control the Indriyas and the mind and to practise Japa Yoga and worship uninterruptedly! May you have unshakable faith in the miraculous powers and marvellous benefits of Japa Yoga! May you all realise the glory of Nama, the Name of God! May you all spread the glory of Nama throughout the length and breadth of the land! Victory to Hari and His Name! Glory to Hari and His Name! May the blessings of Lord Siva, Hari, Rama and Krishna be upon you all!

CONTENTS

Chapter Four
SADHANA

Chapter Five
STORIES OF JAPA-YOGINS

APPENDIX

JAPA YOGA

Chapter One

PHILOSOPHY OF JAPA

1. What Is Japa?

Japa is the repetition of any Mantra or Name of the Lord. In this Kali Yuga or iron age when the physique of the vast majority of persons is not good, rigid Hatha Yogic practices are very difficult. Japa is an easy way to God-realisation. Tukaram of Deo, a Maharashtra saint, Dhruva, Prahlada, Valmiki Rishi, Ramakrishna Paramahamsa—all had attained salvation by uttering the Name of God.

Japa is an important Anga of Yoga. In the Gita you will find "*Yajnanam Japa-Yajnosmi*—Among Yajnas, I am Japa-Yajna." In Kali Yuga the practice of Japa alone can give eternal Peace, Bliss and Immortality. Japa ultimately results in Samadhi or communion with the Lord. Japa must become habitual and must be attended with Sattvic or Divine Bhava, purity, Prema and Sraddha. There is no Yoga greater than Japa Yoga. It can give you all Ishta-Siddhis (whatever you want), Bhakti and Mukti.

Japa is repetition of the Mantra. Dhyana is meditation on the form of the Lord with His attributes. This is the difference between Japa and Dhyana. There is meditation or Dhyana with Japa (Japa-Sahita); there is meditation or Dhyana without Japa (Japa-Rahita). In the beginning you should combine Dhyana with Japa. As you advance the Japa drops by itself; meditation only remains. It is advanced stage. You can then practise concentration separately. You can do whatever you like best in this respect. Om is both Saguna and Nirguna, manifested and unmanifested Brahman. If you are a devotee of Rama you can repeat 'Om Ram' for worship of the manifested Brahman.

Name (Nama) and the object (Rupa) signified by the Name are inseparable. Thought and word are inseparable. Whenever you think of the name of your son, his figure stands before your mental eye, and *vice versa*. Even so when you do Japa of Rama or Krishna, the picture of Rama or Krishna will come before your mind. Therefore Japa and Dhyana go together. They are inseparable.

While you are doing the Japa of any Mantra, think that you are really praying to your Ishta Devata, that your Ishta Devata is really listening to you, that He is looking at you with merciful or graceful eyes, and that He with open hands is giving you full Abhaya-Dana (asking you to be free from all fears whatsoever) with a view to give you your desired object (Moksha). Entertain this Bhava.

Do the Japa with feeling. Know the meaning of the Mantra. Feel His presence in everything and everywhere. Draw closer and nearer to Him when you repeat the Mantra. Think He is shining in the chambers of your heart. He is witnessing your repetition of the Mantra as He is the witness of your mind.

One must take to Japa or Nama-Smarana (remembering the Name of the Lord) very seriously and sincerely with full faith. The chanting of His Name is but serving Him. You must have the same flow of love and respect (devotion) in your heart at the time of thinking of or remembering His Name as that you naturally may have in your heart at the time when you really see Him. You should have full faith and belief in the eternity of the Name.

2. Mantra Yoga

Mantra Yoga is an exact science. *"Mananat trayate iti mantrah*—by the Manana (constant thinking or recollection) of which one is protected or is released from the round of births and deaths, is Mantra." That is called Mantra by the meditation (Manana) on which the Jiva or the individual soul attains freedom from sin, enjoyment in heaven and final liberation, and by the aid of which it attains in full the fourfold fruit (Chaturvarga), i.e., Dharma, Artha, Kama and Moksha. A Mantra is so called because it is achieved by the mental process. The root 'Man' in the word Mantra comes from the first syllable of that word, meaning 'to think' and 'Tra' from 'Trai' meaning 'to protect' or 'free' from the bondage of Samsara or the phenomenal world. By the combination of 'Man' and 'Tra' comes Mantra which calls forth the four aims of being (Chaturvarga) viz., Dharma, Artha, Kama and Moksha.

A Mantra is Divinity. It is divine power or Daivi Sakti manifesting in a sound body. The Mantra itself is Devata. The aspirant should try his level best to realise his unity with the Mantra of the Divinity, and to the extent he does so, the Mantra-power or the Mantra-Sakti supplements his worship-power (Sadhana-Sakti). Just as a flame is strengthened by winds, so also the aspirant's individual Sakti is strengthened by Mantra-Sakti, and then the individual Sakti joins with the Mantra-Sakti to make it more powerful.

The Mantra is awakened from its sleep through the Sadhana-Sakti of the aspirant. The Mantra of the Devata is that letter or combination of letters, which reveals the Deity to the consciousness of the aspirant who has evoked it by the Sadhana-Sakti. The Mantra is a mass of radiant Tejas or energy. Mantra awakens supernatural powers.

A Mantra accelerates, generates creative force. Spiritual life needs harmony in all parts of our being. The whole being must be in perfect ease and in tune with the Divine. Then only the spiritual Truth can be realised. Mantra produces harmony. A Mantra has the power of releasing the cosmic and the supercosmic consciousness. It bestows on the Sadhaka illumination, freedom, supreme Peace, eternal Bliss and Immortality. A Mantra when constantly repeated awakens the consciousness (Chit or Chaitanya). Consciousness or Chaitanya is latent in a Mantra.

Sound exists in four fundamental states, viz., (1) Vaikhari or dense, audible sound, sound in its maximum differentiation; (2) Madhyama or an inner, subtle, more ethereal state at which it is inaudible to physical ear; (3) Pasyanti, a still higher, inner, more ethereal state; (4) Para which represents Isvara-Sakti and is the potential (Karana) state of the sound which is Avyakta or undifferentiated. The Para sound is not, like the Vaikhari, different in different languages. It is the unchanging primal substratum of them all, the source of the universe.

The Japa of a Mantra can bring the practitioner realisation of his highest goal even though he has no knowledge of the meaning of the Mantra. Only it will take a little more time. There is an indescribable power or Achintya Sakti in the Name of God or Mantra. If you repeat the Mantra with concentration on its meaning you will attain God-consciousness quickly.

The repetition of the Mantra removes the dirt of the mind such as lust, anger, greed, etc. Just as the mirror acquires the power of reflection when the dirt covering it is removed, even so the mind from which the impurities have been removed, acquires the capacity to reflect the higher spiritual Truth. Just as soap cleanses the cloth of its impurities, so also, the Mantra is a spiritual soap cleansing the mind. Just as fire cleanses gold of its impurities, so also Mantra cleanses the mind of its impurities. Even a little recitation of a Mantra with Sraddha, Bhava and concentration on its meaning with one-pointed mind, destroys all impurities of the mind. You should utter the Name of God or any Mantra regularly every day. The recital of a Mantra destroys your sins and brings everlasting peace, infinite bliss, prosperity and Immortality. There is not the least doubt about this.

3. Sound and Image

Sounds are vibrations. They give rise to definite forms. Each sound produces a form in the invisible world, and combinations of sound create complicated shapes. The text-books of science describe certain experiments which show that notes produced by certain instruments trace out on a bed of sand definite geometrical figures. It is thus demonstrated that rhythmical vibrations give rise to regular geometrical figures. The Hindu books on music tell us that the various musical tunes, 'Ragas' and 'Raginis', have each a particular shape, which these books graphically describe. For instance, the Megha-Raga is said to be a majestic figure seated on an elephant. The Vasanta-Raga is described as a beautiful youth decked with flowers. All this means that a particular *Raga* or *Ragini*, when accurately sung, produces serial etheric vibrations which create the particular shape, said to be the characteristic of it. This view has recently received corroborations from the experiments carried on by Mrs. Watts Hughes, the gifted author of "Voice Figure". She delivered an illustrated lecture before a select audience in Lord Leighton's studio to demonstrate the beautiful scientific discoveries on which she has alighted, as the result of many years' patient labour. Mrs.

Hughes sings into a simple instrument called an 'Eidophone' which consists of a tube, a receiver and a flexible membrane, and she finds that each note assumes a definite and constant shape, as revealed through a sensitive and mobile medium. At the outset of her lecture, she placed tiny seeds upon the flexible membrane and the air-vibrations set up by the notes she sounded danced them into definite geometric patterns. Afterwards she used dusts of various kinds, copodium dust being found particularly suitable. A reporter, describing the shape of the notes, speaks of them as remarkable revelations of geometry, perspective and shading: "Stars, spirals, snakes and imaginations rioting in a wealth of captivating methodical design." Such were what were first shown. Once when Mrs. Hughes was singing a note, a daisy appeared and disappeared and "I tried," she said, "to sing it back for weeks before; at last I succeeded." Now she knows that precise inflections of the particular note that is a daisy, and it is made constant and definite by a strange method of coaxing an alteration of crescendo and diminuendo. After the audience had gazed enraptured a series of daisies, some with succeeding rows of petals, delicately viewed, they were shown other notes and these were daisies of great beauty. "How wonderful! How lovely!" were the audible exclamations that arose from the late Lord Leighton's studio, an exquisite form succeeded exquisite forms on the screen! The flowers were followed by sea-monsters, serpentine forms of swelling rotundity, full of light and shade and details, feeding in miles of perspective. After these notes came there forms of other trees, trees with fruits falling, trees with a foreground of rocks, trees with sea behind. "Why", exclaimed the people in the audience, "they are just like Japanese landscapes."

While in France, Madame Finlang's singing of a hymn to Virgin Mary "O Ave Marium" brought out the form of Mary with child Jesus on her lap and again the singing of a hymn to 'Bhairava' by a Bengali student of Varanasi studying in France, gave rise to the formation of the figure of Bhairava with his vehicle, the dog.

Thus, repeated singing of the Name of the Lord builds up gradually the form of the Devata or the special manifestation of the Deity whom you seek to worship, and this acts as a focus to concentrate the benign influence of the Divine Being, which radiating from the centre, penetrates the worshipper.

When one enters the state of meditation, the flow of the inner Vritti is greatly intensified. The deeper one goes into meditation the more marked is the effect. The concentration of the mind upwards sends a rush of this force through the top of the head and the response comes in a fine rain of soft magnetism. The feeling arising from the downward power sends a wonderful glow through the body, and one feels as if he is bathed in a soft kind of electricity.

The above experiments demonstrate the following facts:

1. Sounds produce shapes.

2. Particular notes give rise to particular forms.

3. If you want to generate a particular form, you must produce a definite note in a particular pitch.

The repetition of the Panchakshara Mantra, 'Om Namah Sivaya' produces the form of Lord Siva. The repetition of 'Om Namo Narayanaya,' the Ashtakshara Mantra of Vishnu, produces the form of Vishnu. In a Mantra, the vibrations to be produced by the notes are all important. Much emphasis is laid on the pitch (Svara) as well as form (Varna) of a Mantra. Varna literally means colour. In the invisible world all sounds are accompanied by colours, so that they give rise to many-hued shapes. In the same way colours are accompanied by sounds. A particular note has to be used to produce a particular form. Different notes in different pitches give rise to different shapes. In the science of Mantras, we use different Mantras for the purpose of invoking different gods. If you worship Lord Siva you use 'Om Namah Sivaya,' but in worshipping Vishnu or Sakti you will have to change the Mantra. What happens when a Mantra is recited? The repeated recitation of the Mantra produces in the mind the form of the Devata or the Deity connected with the Mantra which is your Ishta, and this form becomes the centre of your consciousness when you directly realise it. It is, therefore, said that the Mantra of the Deva is the Deva himself. This may explain the much misunderstood dictum of the Mimamsa philosophers that the gods do not exist apart from the Mantras (*Mantratmako Devah*). This really means that when a particular Mantra appropriated to a particular god is properly recited, the vibrations so set up, create in the higher planes a special form which that god ensouls for the time being.

Chapter Two

GLORY OF THE NAME

1. Nama Mahima

What a lot of joy the repetition of His Name brings! What a lot of power it infuses into man! How it changes the human nature marvellously! How it exalts a man to the status of divinity! How it destroys old sins, Vasanas, Sankalpas, whims, fancies, depressing moods, sex-impulses and various Samskaras!

How sweet is God's Name! What a tremendous power it possesses! How it transforms quickly the Asuric, diabolical nature into Sattvic, Divine nature! How it brings you face to face with the Lord and makes you realise your oneness with Him (Para Bhakti—Supreme Love)!

The Name of God chanted correctly or incorrectly, knowingly or unknowingly, carefully or carelessly, is sure to give the desired result. The Glory of the Name of God cannot be established through reasoning and intellect. It can certainly be experienced or realised only through devotion, faith and constant repetition of the Name. Every Name is filled with countless potencies or Saktis. The power of the Name is ineffable. Its Glory is indescribable. The efficacy and inherent Sakti of the Name of God in unfathomable.

Just as fire has the natural property of burning inflammable things, so also the Name of God has the power of burning sins, Samskaras and Vasanas and bestowing Eternal Bliss and everlasting peace on those who repeat it. Just as burning quality is natural to and inherent in fire, so also the power of destroying sins with their very root and branch, and bringing the aspirant into blissful union with the Lord through Bhava-Samadhi is natural to and inherent in the Name of God.

O Man! Take refuge in the Name. Nami and Nama are inseparable. Sing the Lord's Name incessantly. Remember the Name of the Lord with every incoming and outgoing breath. In this iron age Nama-Smarana or Japa is the easiest, quickest, safest and surest way to reach god and attain Immortality and perennial Joy. Glory to the Lord! Glory to His Name!

It was the utterance of the Name of God alone that caused the salvation of a great sinner of the type of Ajamila. Ajamila was a righteous Brahmin in the beginning. He fell in love with a low-caste girl and committed many atrocious crimes. It was at the time of death he uttered the name of his son 'Narayana' and there came the Parshadas of Narayana Himself to his rescue, and he (Ajamila) was released from this world for ever. Mark here the extraordinary power of the Name.

You may be aware how the Ganika (prostitute) Pingala was mysteriously transformed into a saintly lady by the power of the Name (repeating the Name of Sri Rama) through her Guru, the parrot which she obtained as a lovely present from a thief, and how she easily obtained salvation. the parrot was trained to utter the Name "Sri Rama, Sri Rama". Pingala knew nothing of Rama-Nama. She heard the sound Rama-Rama through the mouth of the parrot. It was very melodious and charming. Pingala was very much attracted. She fixed her mind on Rama-Nama, uttered by the parrot, and mysteriously entered into Bhava Samadhi (union with Rama). Such is the power of the Name of the Lord. It is a pity that the present-day people who have studied science and who brag of their worthless secular learning have no faith in Nama-Smarana. It is highly deplorable.

Just hear the glory of Rama-Nama. You must learn to take the Name of Rama with full devotion and faith. When you study the Ramayana of Tulasidas you will learn how great the Divine Power of that blessed Name is.

Gandhiji writes: "You might ask me why I tell you to use the word Rama and not one of the many other Names of the Creator. True His Names are as many as and more than the leaves on a tree, and I might, for instance, ask you to use the word God. But what meaning, what associations, would it have for you here? In order to enable you to feel anything when repeating the word God, I should have to teach you some English. I should have to explain to you foreign people's thoughts and associations.

"But in telling you to repeat the Name of Rama, I am giving you a Name worshipped since countless generations by the people of this land—a Name familiar to the very animals and birds, the very trees and stones of Hindusthan, through many thousand years. You will learn from Ramayana how a stone by the roadside sprang to life at the touch of Rama's foot as he passed by. You must learn to repeat the blessed Name of Rama with sweetness and such devotion that the birds will pause in their singing to listen to you, that the very trees will bend their leaves towards you, stirred by the divine melody of that Name."

Kamal got a severe scolding from his father Kabir for prescribing to a rich merchant Rama-Nama to be repeated twice for curing leprosy. Kamal asked the merchant to repeat Rama-Nama twice and yet he was not cured of the disease. Kamal reported to his father this incidence. Kabir was very much annoyed and told Kamal: "You have brought disgrace on me by asking the merchant to repeat Rama-Nama twice. Repetition of Rama-Nama once is quite sufficient. Now beat the merchant severely with a stick on his head. Ask him to stand in the Ganga and repeat Rama-Nama once from the bottom of his heart." Kamal followed the instruction of his father. He gave a good thrashing on the head of the merchant. The merchant repeated Rama-Nama once only with Bhava, from the bottom of his heart. He was completely cured of leprosy.

Kabir sent Kamal to Tulasidas. In the presence of Kamal, Tulasidas wrote Rama-Nama on a Tulasi-leaf and sprinkled the juice over 50 lepers. All were cured. Kamal was quite astonished. Then Kabir sent Kamal to blind Sur Das. Sur Das asked Kamal to bring the corpse that was floating in the river. The corpse was brought. Sur Das repeated 'Ram' only once (not the full Name Rama) in one ear of the corpse, and it was brought back to life. Kamal's heart was filled with awe and wonder. Such is the power of God's Name. My dear friends! My educated college youths! My dear Barristers, Professors, Doctors and Judges! Don't be puffed up with your false secular learning. Repeat the Name of the Lord with Bhava and Prema from the bottom of your heart and realise the Supreme Bliss, Knowledge, Peace and Immortality right now in this very birth, nay, this very second.

Kabir says: "If anyone utters 'Rama' 'Rama' even in dream, I would like to make for his daily use a pair of shoes out of my skin." Who can describe the glory of God's sacred Name? Who can really comprehend the greatness and splendour of the holy Names of God? Even Parvati, the consort of Lord Siva, failed to describe in adequate terms the grandeur and true significance of God's Name. When one sings His Name or hears it sung, he is unconsciously raised to sublime spiritual heights. He loses his body-consciousness. He is immersed in joy. He drinks the divine nectar of Immortality. He gets Divine intoxication. Repetition of God's Name enables the devotee to feel the Divine Presence, the Divine glory, the Divine consciousness within himself and also everywhere. How sweet is Hari's Name! How powerful is the Name of the Lord! How much joy, peace and strength His Name brings to one who repeats it! Blessed indeed are those who repeat God's Name, for they will be free from the wheel of birth and death and will attain Immortality!

The Pandavas were never burnt to death, though the Lakshagriha (house of lac) in which they lived was burnt, because of their immense faith in the Name of Hari; the Gopalakas were not harmed by fire, when the wild fire broke out, because of their immense faith in the Lord's Name; Hanuman was never burnt though his tail was set fire to by the Rakshasas, on account of his immense faith in Rama's Name; Prahlada was not burnt by fire because he had taken refuge in the Name of Hari; Sita was not harmed through fire though she had to undergo the fire-trial for testing her chastity, because she had Rama's Name as her sole refuge; the palace of Vibhishana was not burnt when the whole of Lanka was burnt to ashes, because of his immense faith in the Name of Sri Rama. Such is the glory of the Lord's Name.

2. Benefits of Japa

I

Japa checks the force of the thought-current moving towards objects. It forces the mind to move towards God, towards the attainment of eternal bliss. It eventually helps to have Darsana of God. The Mantra Chaitanya is hidden in every Mantra. Whenever the Sadhaka or spiritual aspirant shows lack of vigour in his Sadhana, the Mantra-Sakti or power of the Mantra reinforces the Sadhana-Sakti of the Sadhaka. Constant and prolonged repetition for some months cuts new grooves in the mind and the brain.

During Japa all the divine qualities steadily flow into your mind from the Lord, just as oil flows from one vessel to another vessel. Japa transforms the nature of the mind. It fills the mind with Sattva.

Japa changes the mental substance from passion to purity, from Rajas to Sattva. It calms and strengthens the mind. It makes the mind introspective. It checks the out-going tendencies of the mind. It eradicates all kinds of evil thoughts and inclinations. It induces determination and austerity. Eventually it leads to the direct Darsana of God, the Ishta Devata, or tutelary Deity, or to God-realisation.

The mind is purified by constant Japa and worship. It is filled with good and pure thoughts. Repetition of Mantra and worship strengthen the good Samskaras. "As a man thinks, so he becomes." This is the psychological law. The mind of a man who trains himself in thinking good, holy thoughts, develops a tendency to think of good thoughts. His character is moulded and transformed by continued good thoughts. When the mind thinks of the image of the Lord during Japa and worship, the mental substance actually assumes the form of the image. The impression of the object is left in the mind. This is called Samskara. When the act is repeated very often, the Samskaras gain strength by repetition and a tendency or habit is formed in the mind. He who entertains thoughts of Divinity becomes transformed actually into the Divinity itself by constant thinking and meditation. His Bhava or disposition is purified and divinised. The meditator and the meditated, the worshipper and the worshipped, the thinker and the thought, become one and the same. This is Samadhi. This is the fruit of worship or Upasana or doing Japa.

Silent repetition of God's Name, HARI OM, or SRI RAMA, is a tremendous tonic and potent specific for all diseases. It should never be stopped even for a day under any circumstances. It is like food. It is a spiritual food for the hungry soul. Lord Jesus says: "You can hardly live on bread alone; but you can live on the Name of God alone." You can drink and live on the nectar that flows during Japa and meditation. Even simple mechanical repetition of a Mantra has got very great effect. It purifies the mind. It serves as a gate-keeper. It gives intimations to you whenever some worldly thoughts enter the mind. At once you can drive those thoughts and do Smarana of the Mantra. Even during mechanical repetition, a portion of the mind is there at work with it.

If you utter the word 'excreta' or 'urine' when your friend is taking his meals, he may at once vomit his food. If you think of 'Garam Pakoda', 'hot Pakoda', your tongue will get salivation. There is a Sakti in every word. When such is the case with ordinary words, how much more power or Sakti should there be in the Name of God—HARI, RAMA, SIVA or KRISHNA? Repetition or thinking of His Name produces a tremendous influence on the mind. It transforms the mental substance, 'Chitta', overhauls the vicious old Samskaras in the mind, transmutes the Asuric or diabolical nature and brings the devotee face to face with God. There is no doubt about this. O sceptics and scientific atheists! Wake up! Open your eyes. Chant His Name always. Sing. Do Kirtan.

It is only 'Nama-Smarana' that is free from difficulties and troubles. It is easy, comfort-giving and simple. It is therefore said to be the 'head', the 'King' of all Sadhanas (means to God-realisation).

When you repeat His Name, you must evince from the bottom of your heart Ananya Bhakti (unflinching devotion to God without love for any other object). You must drive off all other worldly thoughts from your mind. Fill the mind with thoughts of God and God alone. You must struggle. You must exert hard. Remain absorbed in Him. You must have Avyabhicharini Bhakti.

To love Lord Krishna for 3 months, Rama for another 3 months, Sakti for 6 months, Hanuman for some time, Lord Siva for some time, is not good. This is Vyabhicharini Bhakti. If you love Krishna, Love Him alone till the end. Just as you see wood alone at the back of chair, table, bench, stick, almirah, cup-board, etc., see the Antaratman, Avyakta (hidden) Krishna alone in a flower, tree, fruits, tumbler, and all objects. This is Ananya Bhakti. This is Para Bhakti.

Just as you remember all the qualities of your son when you think of his name, e.g., Visvanathan, you should remember the qualities of God as Omnipotence, Omniscience, etc., when you think of His Name.

When you repeat the Mantra, have Sattvic Bhava or Suddha Bhava (right mental Attitude, Sattvic feeling). The Bhava comes slowly when the purification-process goes on. Even mere mechanical repetition has very great effect. The vibration in the mind set up by the repetition purifies the Chitta (mind-stuff), brings Chitta-Suddhi.

A beginner should have a Japa-Maala or rosary. Later on he can take recourse to Manasika Japa (mental repetition). If a man repeats the Mantra for 6 hours daily, his heart will be purified quickly. He can feel the purity. You must have great faith in your Guru-Mantra. You must keep it a secret, also.

The shorter the Mantra you use, the greater will be your power of concentration. Of all Mantras Rama-Nama is the best. It is easy to repeat also.

II

Japa purifies the heart.
Japa steadies the mind.
Japa destroys the Shadripus (six enemies).
Japa destroys birth and death.
Japa burns sins.
Japa scorches Samskaras.
Japa annihilates attachment.
Japa induces Vairagya.
Japa roots out all desires.
Japa makes one fearless.
Japa removes delusion.
Japa gives supreme Peace.
Japa develops Prema.
Japa unites the devotee with the Lord.
Japa gives health, wealth, strength and long life.
Japa brings God-consciousness.

Japa bestows Eternal Bliss.
Japa awakens the Kundalini.

III

Japa gives a nice, refreshing, exhilarating, spiritual bath.
It wonderfully washes the subtle body or
Linga Sarira or astral body.
Japa is a marvellous divine soap for the mind.
It cleanses it of its various kinds of impurities.
If you are not able to form the image of your Ishta Devata,
If you are not able to fix the mind on your tutelary Deity,
You may try to hear the sound of the Mantra repeated by you,
Or think of the letters of the Mantra in order.
This will stop mind-wandering.

IV

At any moment death will snatch you away.
For eating and drinking this life is not meant.
Very difficult it is to get a human birth,
O friend, wake up, do Japa of Hari Om or Sri Rama.
There is no better healer in this iron age
Than the Japa of the Mantra of God.
Japa keeps Lord Yama away.
Japa destroys the five afflictions and three Taapas.
Just as fire burns cotton,
So does Japa burn all Karmas,
Just as the Ganga purifies a dirty cloth,
So does Japa purify the dirty mind.
The eager aspirant thirsting for God's Darsana
Punctually gets up at Brahmamuhurta,
With crossed legs in Padmasana he sits.
With Bhava and Prema the beads he rolls,
Silent Japa does he sometimes,
Whispers or hums he at other times,
Though near, his neighbour can't hear.
Sometimes loud Japa does he when the mind wanders.
Anushthana he performs on the banks of the Ganga,
Lives on milk and fruits or fasts sometimes,
Finishes Purascharana of Japa of lakhs,
Gets peace of mind and divine experiences.
Havan he does when Purascharana is over,
The Brahmins, the Sadhus, the poor he feeds.

Thus pleases he the Lord and gets His Grace,
And attains Bliss, Perfection and Immortality!
The fire of Japa imparts divine splendour to his face.
The Japa-Yogi now shines more resplendent than the Sun,
Through Japa alone all Siddhis and Riddhis he attains,
Even Adi-Sesha cannot now describe his splendour and glory.

Chapter Three

MANTRAS

1. Pranava

Om (Aum) is everything. Om is the Name or symbol of God, Isvara, Brahman. Om is your real name. Om covers the whole threefold experience of man. Om stands for all the phenomenal worlds. From Om this sense-universe has been projected. The world exists in Om and dissolves in Om. 'A' represents the physical plane. 'U' represents the mental and astral plane, the world of intelligent spirits, all heavens. 'M' represents the whole deep sleep state, and all that is unknown even in your wakeful state, all that is beyond the reach of the intellect. Om represents all. Om is the basis of your life, thought and intelligence. Om is everything. All words which denote objects are centred in Om. Hence the whole world has come from Om, rests in Om, and dissolves in Om. As soon as you sit for meditation, chant Om loudly 3 or 6 or 12 times. This will drive away all worldly thoughts from the mind and remove *Vikshepa* (tossing of mind). Then take to mental repetition of Om.

The Japa of Om (Pranava Japa) has a tremendous influence on the mind. The pronunciation of the sacred syllable Om, is one which had engaged the attention of all Europeans devoted to Eastern studies. The vibrations set up by this word are so powerful that, if one persists in taking recourse to them, they would bring the largest building to the ground. This seems difficult to believe in until one has tried the practice; but once having tried it one can easily understand how the above statement may be true and perfectly correct. I have tested the power of the vibrations and can quite believe that the effect would be as stated. Pronounced as spelt, it will have a certain effect upon the student; but pronounced in its correct method, it arouses and transforms every atom in his physical body, setting up new vibrations and conditions, and awakening the sleeping power of the body.

2. Hari Nama

Every Mantra has the following six parts: It has got a *Rishi* who had Self-realisation for the first time through this Mantra and who gave this Mantra to others. He is the Seer for this Mantra. Sage Visvamitra is the Rishi for Gayatri. It has a *Metre* also. There is a particular *Devata* or presiding Deity of the Mantra. It has got a *Bija* or seed. This gives a special power to the Mantra. This is the essence of the Mantra. Every Mantra has got a *Sakti*. Lastly it has a *Kilaka* (Pillar or pin). This plugs the Mantra-Chaitanya that is hidden in the Mantra. As soon as the plug is removed by constant and prolonged repetition of the Name, the Chitanya that is hidden is revealed. The devotee gets Darsana of the Ishta Devata.

"Mananat trayate iti mantrah"—By the Manana (constant thinking or recollection) of which one is protected or is released is Mantra. It is Mantra that leads to the realisation of one's own Ishta Devata. And also, practically speaking, the Ishta Devata and the Mantra are one and the same thing.

The mere remembrance of Hari's Name destroys all the accumulated sins of various births.

"Harer-Nama Harer-Nama Harer-Namaiva Kevalam; Kalau Nastyeva Nastyeva Nastyeva Gatiranyatha." In this Kali Yuga, there exists only the Name of Hari, Hari, Hari. In this Kali Yuga, there is on other means, no other way, and no other method for attaining salvation. Even the sins of the greatest of the sinners are brought to nothing by the utterance of Hari's Name (Name of God). Not only this, but by doing so, we get eternal safety, Self-realisation and eternal happiness. This is the importance of Hari-Nama.

"Rama Na Sakahin Nama Gun Gai—Even Rama, God Himself, cannot describe the greatness of Nama." Then what to speak of us? It is all the more needed at this present age of ours. Because in this Kali Yuga (iron age): *"Kali Yuga Kevala Nama Adhara*—The only support in this iron age or Kali Yuga is nothing but the Name of God." There is no other means, simpler and easier than this, to obtain eternal happiness and peace.

"Rama Nama Manideep Dharu Jiha Dehari Dwar,
Tulsi Bhitar Baher Hun Jo Chahasi Ujiyar."

Put this jewel, light of Rama-Nama (the Name of Rama) at the gate of your door, tongue, if you want to illuminate yourself, both inside and outside ('in' and 'out' of your own self).

"Ulta Naam Japat Jag Jana,
Valmiki Bhaye Brahma Samana."

All the world knows that by uttering the Name even in its opposite form, by saying Mara-Mara instead of Rama-Rama, the great saint Valmiki became Brahman Himself.

When such is the effect of Ulta Nama, then who can speak of the glory of the right and the proper Nama (Name)?

"Gafil Tu Hai Ghadyal Yah Deta Hai Munadi
Gardoon ne Ghadi Umar Ki Teri Aur Ghata di."

O careless one! The bell is reminding you again and again. The time has but brought you near the limit of your life-time. And therefore:

"Ram Naam ki Loot Hai, Loot Sake To Loot,
Anta Kaal Pachtayega Jab Pran Jayenge Choot."

You must take for yourself in abundance the Name of Sri Rama. Otherwise, at the last moment of your life, when death approaches you, and when Prana (life) will cease to remain in this body of yours, you will but grieve and lament for it.

"Ram Naam Aaradhano Tulsi Britha Na Jay,
Larkayi Ko Pairibo Aage Hot Sahay;
Tulsi Apne Ram Ko Reejh Bhajo Ya Kheej,
Ulta Seedha Jaamihain Khet Pare Te Beej."

The well-known poet Goswami Tulsidasji says: "The worshipping of the Name of Rama never goes in vain, just as the practice of swimming in one's boyhood is of great help at some future time." He says that whether you remember Rama in your pleasant mood, or unpleasant mood, it is sure to give its good effect, just as the seeds in the fields thrown either rightly or wrongly give good results.

Those who do not believe in this may do this for the sake of examination or test and then do as they like or think proper. It is not at all wise to while away the time in arguments or vain discussions merely. Life is short. Time is fleeting. The body is continually decaying. There is nothing but gain and gain only in doing Japa or Nama-Smarana.

3. Kali-Santarana Upanishad

At the end of Dvapara Yuga Narada Rishi approached Brahma, the Creator, and asked: "O Lord! How shall I be able to cross Kali, wandering in this world?" Brahma replied: "Hearken that which the Srutis keep as secret and hidden, by which one may cross the Samsara in Kali Yuga. One can shake off the evil effects of Kali through mere uttering of the Name of Lord Narayana." Again Narada asked: "May I know the Name, my Lord?" Brahma replied:

"Hare Rama Hare Rama Rama Rama Hare Hare,
Hare Krishna Hare Krishna Krishna Krishna Hare Hare."

These 16 Names destroy, doubtless, the evil effects of Kali. They remove the Avarana or veil of ignorance of the Jiva surrounded by 16 Kalas (rays). Then, like the sun which shines in full effulgence after the clouds are dispersed, Para Brahman alone shines in full splendour.

Narada asked: "O Lord! May I know the rules to be observed in the repetition of the Mantras?" Brahma replied: "There are no rules. Whoever in a pure or in an impure state utters these always, attains *Salokya* (the same world of), *Samipya* (proximity with), *Sarupya* (the same form of) or *Sayujya* (absorption into) Brahman."

Whoever utters 3½ crores (35 millions) of times this Mantra composed of 16 Names gets rid even of the sin of the murder of a Brahmin. He becomes purified from the sin of thefts of gold. He becomes purified from the sin of cohabitation with a woman of a low caste. He is purified of the sins of wrong done to Pitris, Devas and men. Having given up all Dharmas, he becomes freed at once from all sins. He is at once released from all bondages and gets Mukti. This is the Kali-Santarana Upanishad of the Krishna-Yajur-Veda. In Bengal this Mantra is repeated by a large number of people. It is the favourite Mantra of the Vaishnavites of Bengal.

4. Japa Vidhana

Japa is the repetition of any Mantra or Name of the Lord with Bhava and feeling.

Japa removes the impurities of the mind, destroys sins and brings the devotee face to face with the Lord.

Every Name is filled with countless powers. Just as fire has the natural property of burning things, so also the Name of God has the power of burning sins and desires.

Sweeter than all sweet things, more auspicious than all good things, purer than all pure things, is the Name of the Lord.

The Name of the Lord is a boat to cross this Samsara. It is a weapon to destroy the mind.

The repetition of a Mantra again and again generates great spiritual force and momentum and intensifies the spiritual Ṣamskaras or impressions.

Repetition of a Mantra raises vibrations. Vibrations give rise to definite forms. Repetition of 'Om Namah Sivaya' gives rise to the form of Lord Siva in the mind; repetition of 'Om Namo Narayanaya' gives rise to the form of Lord Hari.

The glory of the Name of God cannot be established through reasoning and intellect. It can certainly be experienced or realised, only through devotion, faith and constant repetition.

Japa is of three kinds, viz., Manasika Japa or mental Japa, Upamsu Japa or Japa with humming, and Vaikhari Japa or loud audible Japa.

Mental repetition or Japa or Manasika Japa is more powerful than loud Japa.

Get up at 4 a.m., and do the Japa for two hours. Brahmamuhurta is most favourable for Japa and meditation.

If you cannot take bath, wash your hands, feet, face and body, and sit for Japa.

Face the North or the East when sitting. This enhances the efficacy of the Japa.

Sit on Kusa-grass or deer-skin or rug. Spread a sheet of cloth over it. This conserves body-electricity.

Do some prayer before starting the Japa.

Have a steady pose. Have Asana-Jaya or conquest over Asana. You must be able to sit on Padma, Siddha or Sukha Asana for three hours at a stretch.

When you repeat the Mantra, have the feeling or mental attitude that the Lord is seated in your heart, that Sattva or purity is flowing from the Lord to your mind, that the Mantra purifies your heart, destroys desires and cravings and evil thoughts.

Do not do the Japa in a hurried manner, as a contractor tries to finish his work in a hurried way. Do it slowly with Bhava, one-pointedness of mind and single-minded devotion.

Pronounce the Mantra distinctly and without mistakes. Do not repeat it too fast or too slow.

Use not the index finger while rolling the beads. Use the thumb, the middle and the ring fingers. When counting of one Maala is over, revert it and come back again. Cross not the Meru. Cover your hand with a towel.

Be vigilant. Keep an alert attention during Japa. Stand up and do the Japa when sleep tries to overpower you.

Resolve to finish a certain minimum number of Maalas before leaving the seat.

Maala or rosary is a whip to goad the mind towards God.

Sometimes do the Japa without Maala. Go by the watch.

Practise meditation also along with Japa. This is Japa-Sahita-Dhyana. Gradually Japa will drop and meditation alone will continue. This is Japa-Rahita-Dhyana.

Have four sittings for Japa daily—early morning, noon, evening and night.

A devotee of Lord Vishnu should repeat 'Om Namo Narayanaya'; a devotee of Lord Siva 'Om Namah Sivaya'; a devotee of Lord Krishna 'Om Namo Bhagavate Vaasudevaya'; a devotee of Lord Rama 'Om Sri Ramaya Namah' or 'Om Sri Rama Jaya Rama Jaya Jaya Rama'; a devotee of Devi, Gayatri Mantra or Durga Mantra.

It is better to stick to one Mantra alone. See the Lord Krishna in Rama, Siva, Durga, Gayatri, and everyone.

Regularity in Japa Sadhana is most essential. Sit in the same place and at the same time.

Purascharana is repetition of the Mantra Akshara-Laksha, one lakh times for each letter.

Japa must become habitual. Even in dream you must be doing Japa.

Japa Yoga is the easiest, quickest, safest, surest, and cheapest way for attaining God-realisation. Glory to the Lord! Glory, glory to His Name!

O Man! Take refuge in the Name. Nama and Nami are inseparable.

5. Mantras for Japa

१. ॐ श्रीमहागणपतये नमः

२. ॐ नमः शिवाय

३. ॐ नमो नारायणाय

४. हरिः ॐ

५. हरिः ॐ तत् सत्

६. हरे राम हरे राम राम राम हरे हरे
हरे कृष्ण हरे कृष्ण कृष्ण कृष्ण हरे हरे

७. ॐ नमो भगवते वासुदेवाय

८. ॐ श्रीकृष्णाय गोविन्दाय गोपीजनवल्लभाय नमः

९. ॐ श्रीकृष्णाय नमः

१०. श्रीराम जय राम जय जय राम

११. ॐ श्रीरामाय नमः

१२. ॐ श्रीसीतारामचन्द्राभ्यां नमः

१३. ॐ श्रीराम राम रामेति रमे रामे मनोरमे।
सहस्रनाम तत्तुल्यं राम नाम वरानने॥

१४. आपदामपहर्तारं दातारं सर्वसम्पदाम्।
लोकाभिरामं श्रीरामं भूयो भूयो नमाम्यहम्॥

१५. आर्तानामार्तिहन्तारं भीतानां भीतिनाशनम्।
द्विषतां कालदण्डं तं रामचन्द्रं नमाम्यहम्॥

१६. रामाय रामभद्राय रामचन्द्राय वेधसे।
रघुनाथाय नाथाय सीतायाः पतये नमः॥

१७. सीताराम॥ राधेश्याम॥ राधेकृष्ण॥

१८. ॐ श्रीरामः शरणं मम

१९. ॐ श्रीकृष्णः शरणं मम

२०. ॐ श्रीसीतारामः शरणं मम

२१. ॐ श्रीरामचन्द्रचरणौ शरणं प्रपद्ये

२२. ॐ श्रीमन्नारायणचरणौ शरणं प्रपद्ये

२३. सकृदेव प्रपन्नाय तवास्मीति च याचते।
अभयं सर्वभूतेभ्यो ददाम्येतद् व्रतं मम॥

२४. ॐ श्री हनुमते नमः

२५. ॐ श्रीसरस्वत्यै नमः

२६. ॐ श्री कालिकायै नमः

२७. ॐ श्री दुर्गायै नमः

२८..ॐ श्रीमहालक्ष्म्यै नमः

२९. ॐ श्रीशरवणभवाय नमः

३०. ॐ श्रीत्रिपुरसुन्दर्यै नमः

३१. ॐ श्रीबालापरमेश्वर्यै नमः

३२. ॐ सोऽहम्

३३. ॐ अहं ब्रह्मास्मि

३४. ॐ तत्त्वमसि

३५. ॐ त्र्यम्बकं यजामहे सुगन्धिं पुष्टिवर्धनम्।
उर्वारुकमिव बन्धनान्मृत्योर्मुक्षीय माऽमृतात्॥

* * *

अथ अष्टाक्षरमन्त्रः

ॐ नमो नारायणाय

अस्य श्रीमन्नारायणाष्टाक्षरी महामन्त्रस्य साध्यनारायण ऋषिः। देवीगायत्री छन्दः। श्रीमन्नारायणो देवता।। जपे विनियोगः।।

ॐ क्रुद्धोल्काय स्वाहा अंगुष्ठाभ्यां नमः

ॐ महोल्काय स्वाहा तर्जनीभ्यां नमः

ॐ वीरोल्काय स्वाहा मध्यमाभ्यां नमः

ॐ द्व्युल्काय स्वाहा अनामिकाभ्यां नमः

ॐ ज्ञानोल्काय स्वाहा कनिष्ठिकाभ्यां नमः

ॐ सहस्रोल्काय स्वाहा करतलकरपुष्ठाभ्यां नमः

इति करन्यासः

ॐ क्रुद्धोल्काय स्वाहा हृदयाय नमः

ॐ महोल्काय स्वाहा शिरसे स्वाहा

ॐ वीरोल्काय स्वाहा शिखायै वषट्

ॐ द्व्युल्काय स्वाहा कवचाय हुँ

ॐ ज्ञानोल्काय स्वाहा नेत्रत्रयाय वौषट्

ॐ सहस्रोल्काय स्वाहा अस्त्राय फट्

इत्यङ्गन्यासः

ॐ उद्यत्कोटिदिवाकराभमनिशं शङ्खं गदां पङ्कजं
चक्रं विभ्रतमिन्दिरावसुमतीसंशोभिपार्श्वद्वयम्।
कोटीराङ्गदहारकुण्डलधरं पीताम्बरं कौस्तुभोद्दीप्तं
विश्वधरं स्ववक्षसि लसच्छ्रीवत्सचिह्नं भजे।।

इति ध्यानम्

* * *

अथ द्वादशाक्षरमन्त्रः

ॐ नमो भगवते वासुदेवाय

अस्य श्रीद्वादशाक्षरी महामन्त्रस्य प्रजापतिः ऋषिः। गायत्री छन्दः वासुदेवः परमात्मा देवता।। जपे विनियोगः।।

ॐ नमो नमोऽङ्गुष्ठाभ्यां नमः

ॐ भगवते नमस्तर्जनीभ्यां नमः

ॐ वासुदेवाय नमो मध्यमाभ्यां नमः

ॐ नमो नमोऽनामिकाभ्यां नमः

ॐ भगवते नमः कनिष्ठिकाभ्यां नमः

ॐ वासुदेवाय नमः करतलकरपृष्ठाभ्यां नमः

इति करन्यासः

ॐ नमो नमो हृदयाय नमः

ॐ भगवते नमः शिरसे स्वाहा

ॐ वासुदेवाय नमः शिखायै वषट्

ॐ नमो नमः कवचाय हुँ

ॐ भगवते नमः नेत्रत्रयाय वौषट्

ॐ वासुदेवाय नमोऽस्त्राय फट्

इत्यङ्गन्यासः

ॐ विष्णुं शारदचन्द्रकोटिसदृशं शङ्खं रथाङ्गं गदा-
मंभोजं दधतं सिताब्जनिलयं कान्त्या जगन्मोहनम्।
आबद्धाङ्गदहारकुण्डलमहामौलिं स्फुरत्कङ्कणं
श्रीवत्सांकमुदारकौस्तुभधरं वन्दे मुनीन्द्रैः स्तुतम्।।

इति ध्यानम्

* * *

अथ शिवपञ्चाक्षरमन्त्रः

ॐ नमः शिवाय

अस्य श्रीशिवपञ्चाक्षरी महामन्त्रस्य वामदेव ऋषिः। पंक्तिश्छन्दः। ईशानो (वामदेवो) देवता।। ॐ बीजम्। नमः शक्तिः। शिवायेति कीलकम्। जपे विनियोगः।।

ॐ ॐ अङ्गुष्ठाभ्यां नमः

ॐ नं तर्जनीभ्यां नमः

ॐ मं मध्यमाभ्यां नमः

ॐ शिं अनामिकाभ्यां नमः

ॐ वां कनिष्ठिकाभ्यां नमः

ॐ यं करतलकरपृष्ठाभ्यां नमः

इति करन्यासः

ॐ ॐ हृदयाय नमः

ॐ नं शिरसे स्वाहा

ॐ मं शिखायै वषट्

ॐ शिं कवचाय हुँ

ॐ वां नेत्रत्रयाय वौषट्

ॐ यं अस्त्राय फट्

इत्यङ्गन्यासः

ॐ ध्यायेन्नित्यं महेशं रजतगिरिनिभं चारुचन्द्रावतंसं
रत्नाकल्पोज्ज्वलाङ्गं परशुमृगवराभीतिहस्तं प्रसन्नम्।
पद्मासीनं समन्तात् स्तुतममरगणैर्व्याघ्रकृत्तिं वसानं
विश्वाद्यं विश्वबीजं निखिलभयहरं पञ्चवक्त्रं त्रिनेत्रम्।।

इति ध्यानम्

Transliteration

No	Mantras	Devata
1.	Om Sri Maha-Ganapataye Namah	Lord Ganapati
2.	Om Namassivaya (Panchakshara Mantra)	Lord Siva
3.	Om Namo Narayanaya (Ashtakshara Manta)	Lord Hari
4.	Harih Om	Lord Hari
5.	Harih Om Tat Sat	Lord Hari
6.	Hare Rama Hare Rama, Rama Rama Hare Hare; Hare Krishna Hare Krishna Krishna Krishna Hare Hare	Maha Mantra
7.	Om Namo Bhagavate Vaasudevaya	Lord Krishna
8.	Om Sri Krishnaya Govindaya Gopijana Vallabhaya Namah	Lord Krishna
9.	Om Sri Krishnaya Namah	Lord Krishna
10.	Om Sri Rama, Jaya Rama, Jaya Jaya Rama	Lord Rama
11.	Om Sri Ramaya Namah	Lord Rama
12.	Om Sri Sita-Ramachandrabhyam Namah	Lord Rama
13.	Sri Rama Rama Rameti, Rame Rame Manorame, SahasranamaTattulyam Rama Nama Varanane	Lord Rama
14.	Apadamapaharttaram Dataram Sarvasampadam; Lokabhiramam Sri Ramam Bhuyo Bhuyo Namamyaham	Lord Rama
15.	Artanamartihantaram Bhitanam Bhitinasanam; Dvishatam Kaladandam Tam Ramachandram Namamyaham	Lord Rama
16.	Ramaya Ramabhadraya Ramachandraya Vedhase; Raghunathaya Nathaya Sitayah Pataye Namah	Lord Rama
17.	Sita Ram; Radhe Shyam; Radhe Krishna	Jugal Mantra
18.	Om Sri Ramah Saranam Mama	Saranagati Mantra
19.	Om Sri Krishnah Saranam Mama	Saranagati Mantra
20.	Om Sri Sita-Ramah Saranam Mama	Saranagati Mantra
21.	Om Sri Ramachandra Charanau Saranam Prapadye	Saranagati Mantra
22.	Om Sriman Narayana Charanau Saranam Prapadye	Saranagati Mantra
23.	Sakrideva Prapannaya Tavasmiti Cha Yachate; Abhayam Sarvabhutebhyo Dadamyeytad Vratam Mama	Saranagati Mantra
24.	Om Sri Hanumate Namah	Sri Hanuman
25.	Om Sri Sarasvatyai Namah	Sri Sarasvati
26.	Om Sri Kaalikayai Namah	Sri Kaalika
27.	Om Sri Durgayai Namah	Sri Devi
28.	Om Sri Maha-Lakshmyai Namah	Sri Lakshmi
29.	Om Sri Saravanabhavaya Namah	Lord Subrahmanya or Karttikeya

30. Om Sri Tripura-Sundaryai Namah — Tripura Sundari
31. Om Sri Bala-Paramesvaryai Namah — Sarada
32. Om Soham — Vedantic Formula
33. Om Aham Brahma Asmi — Vedantic Formula
34. Om Tat Tvam Asi — Vedantic Formula
35. Om Tryambakam Yajamahe Sugandhim Pushtivardhanam,
Urvarukamiva Bandhanan-Mrityormukshiya Maamritat

Maha-Mrityunjaya Mantra

GAYATRIS OF DIFFERENT DEVATAS

Ganesa-Gayatri I

१. ॐ एकदन्ताय विद्महे वक्रतुण्डाय धीमहि।
तन्नो दन्ती प्रचोदयात्॥

Ganesa-Gayatri II

२. ॐ तत्पुरुषाय विद्महे वक्रतुण्डाय धीमहि।
तन्नो दन्ती प्रचोदयात्॥

Brahma-Gayatri I

३. ॐ वेदात्मने विद्महे हिरण्यगर्भाय धीमहि।
तन्नो ब्रह्मा प्रचोदयात् ॥

Brahma-Gayatri II

४. ॐ चतुर्मुखाय विद्महे कमण्डलुधराय धीमहि।
तन्नो ब्रह्मा प्रचोदयात् ॥

Vishnu-Gayatri

५. ॐ नारायणाय विद्महे वासुदेवाय धीमहि।
तन्नो विष्णुः प्रचोदयात् ॥

Nrisimha-Gayatri I

६. ॐ वज्रनखाय विद्महे तीक्ष्णदंष्ट्राय धीमहि।
तन्नो नृसिंहः प्रचोदयात् ॥

Nrisimha-Gayatri II

७. ॐ नृसिंहाय विद्महे वज्रनखाय धीमहि।
तन्नः सिंहः प्रचोदयात् ॥

Garuda-Gayatri

८. ॐ तत्पुरुषाय विद्महे सुवर्णपक्षाय धीमहि।
तन्नो गरुडः प्रचोदयात् ॥

Rudra-Gayatri I

९. ॐ तत्पुरुषाय विद्महे महादेवाय धीमहि।
तन्नो रुद्रः प्रचोदयात् ॥

Rudra-Gayatri II

१०. ॐ तत्पुरुषाय विद्महे सहस्राक्षाय महादेवाय धीमहि।
तन्नो रुद्रः प्रचोदयात् ॥

Nandikesvara-Gayatri

११. ॐ तत्पुरुषाय विद्महे नन्दिकेश्वराय धीमहि।
तन्नो वृषभः प्रचोदयात् ॥

Shanmukha-Gayatri I

१२. ॐ तत्पुरुषाय विद्महे महासेनाय धीमहि।
तन्नः स्कन्दः प्रचोदयात् ॥

Shanmukha-Gayatri II

१३. ॐ षण्मुखाय विद्महे महासेनाय धीमहि।
तन्नः षष्ठः प्रचोदयात् ॥

Surya-Gayatri I

१४. ॐ भास्कराय विद्महे महाद्युतिकराय धीमहि।
तन्नः आदित्यः प्रचोदयात् ॥

Surya-Gayatri II

१५. ॐ आदित्याय विद्महे सहस्रकिरणाय धीमहि।
तन्नो भानुः प्रचोदयात् ॥

Surya-Gayatri III

१६. ॐ प्रभाकराय विद्महे दिवाकराय धीमहि।
तन्नः सूर्यः प्रचोदयात् ॥

Durga-Gayatri I

१७. ॐ कात्यायन्यै विद्महे कन्याकुमार्यै धीमहि।
तन्नो दुर्गा प्रचोदयात् ॥

Durga-Gayatri II

१८. ॐ महाशूलिन्यै विद्महे महादुर्गायै धीमहि।
तन्नो भगवती प्रचोदयात् ॥

Rama-Gayatri

१९. ॐ दाशरथये विद्महे सीतावल्लभाय धीमहि।
तन्नो रामः प्रचोदयात् ॥

Hanumad-Gayatri

२०. ॐ आञ्जनेयाय विद्महे वायुपुत्राय धीमहि।
तन्नो हनुमान् प्रचोदयात् ॥

Krishna-Gayatri

२१. ॐ देवकीनन्दनाय विद्महे वासुदेवाय धीमहि।
तन्नः कृष्णः प्रचोदयात् ॥

Gopala-Gayatri

२२. ॐ गोपालाय विद्महे गोपीजनवल्लभाय धीमहि।
तन्नो गोपालः प्रचोदयात् ॥

Parasurama-Gayatri

२३. ॐ जामदग्न्याय विद्महे महावीराय धीमहि।
तन्नः परशुरामः प्रचोदयात् ॥

Dakshinamurti-Gayatri

२४. ॐ दक्षिणामूर्तये विद्महे ध्यानस्थाय धीमहि.
तन्नो धीशः प्रचोदयात् ॥

Guru-Gayatri

२५. ॐ गुरुदेवाय विद्महे परब्रह्मणे धीमहि।
तन्नो गुरुः प्रचोदयात् ॥

Hamsa-Gayatri I

२६. ॐ हंसाय विद्महे परमहंसाय धीमहि।
तन्नो हंसः प्रचोदयात् ॥

Hamsa-Gayatri II

२७. ॐ परमहंसाय विद्महे महातत्त्वाय धीमहि।
तन्नो हंसः प्रचोदयात् ॥

Hayagriva-Gayatri

२८. ॐ वागीश्वराय विद्महे हयग्रीवाय धीमहि।
तन्नो हंसः प्रचोदयात् ॥

Tantrika- (Brahma-)Gayatri

२९. ॐ परमेश्वराय विद्महे परतत्त्वाय धीमहि।
तन्नो ब्रह्म प्रचोदयात् ॥

Sarasvati-Gayatri

३०. ॐ वाग्देव्यै च विद्महे कामराजाय धीमहि।
तन्नो देवी प्रचोदयात् ॥

Lakshmi-Gayatri

३१. ॐ महादेव्यै च विद्महे विष्णुपत्न्यै च धीमहि।
तन्नो लक्ष्मीःप्रचोदयात् ॥

Sakti-Gayatri

३२. ॐ सर्वसंमोहिन्यै विद्महे विश्वजनन्यै धीमहि।
तन्नः शक्तिः प्रचोदयात् ॥

Annapurna-Gayatri

३३. ॐ भगवत्यै च विद्महे महेश्वर्यै च धीमहि।
तन्नोऽन्नपूर्णा प्रचोदयात् ॥

Kaalika-Gayatri

३४. ॐ कालिकायै च विद्महे श्मशानवासिन्यै धीमहि।
तन्नोऽघोरा प्रचोदयात् ॥

Transliteration

1. Om Ekadantaya Vidmahe Vakratundaya Dheemahi, Tanno Danti Prachodayat.

2. Om Tatpurushaya Vidmahe Vakratundaya Dheemahi, Tanno Danti Prachodayat.

3. Om Vedatmane Vidmahe Hiranyagarbhaya Dheemahi, Tanno Brahma Prachodayat.

4. Om Chaturmukhaya Vidmahe Kamandaludharaya Dheemahi, Tanno Brahma Prachodayat.

5. Om Narayanaya Vidmahe Vaasudevaya Dheemahi, Tanno Vishnuh Prachodayat.

6. Om Vajranakhaya Vidmahe Tikshnadamshtraya Dheemahi, Tanno Nrisimha Prachodayat.

7. Om Nrisimhaya Vidmahe Vajranakhaya Dheemahi, Tannah Simhah Prachodayat.

8. Om Tatpurushaya Vidmahe Suvarnapakshaya Dheemahi, Tanno Garudah Prachodayat.

9. Om Tatpurushaya Vidmahe Mahadevaya Dheemahi, Tanno Rudrah Prachodayat.

10. Om Tatpurushaya Vidmahe Shasrakshaya Mahadevaya Dheemahi, Tanno Rudrah Prachodayat.

11. Om Tatpurushaya Vidmahe Nandikesvaraya Dheemahi, Tanno Vrishabhah Prachodayat.

12. Om Tatpurushaya Vidmahe Mahasenaya Dheemahi, Tannah Skandah Prachodayat.

13. Om Shanmukhaya Vidmahe Mahasenaya Dheemahi, Tannah Shashthah Prachodayat.

14. Om Bhaskaraya Vidmahe Mahadyutikaraya Dheemahi, Tannah Adityah Prachodayat.

15. Om Adityaya Vidmahe Sahasrakiranaya Dheemahi, Tanno Bhanuh Prachodayat.

16. Om Prabhakaraya Vidmahe Divakaraya Dheemahi, Tannah Suryah Prachodayat.

17. Om Katyayanyai Vidmahe Kanyakumaryai Dheemahi, Tanno Durga Prachodayat.

18. Oṃ Mahasulinyai Vidmahe Mahadurgayai Dheemahi, Tanno Bhagavatee Prachodayat.

19. Om Daasarathaye Vidmahe Sitavallabhaya Dheemahi, Tanno Ramah Prachodayat.

20. Om Anjaneyaya Vidmahe Vayuputraya Dheemahi, Tanno Hanuman Prachodayat.

21. Om Devakinandanaya Vidmahe Vaasudevaya Dheemahi, Tannah Krishnah Prachodayat.

22. Om Gopalaya Vidmahe Gopijanavallabhaya Dheemahi, Tanno Gopalah Prachodayat.

23. Om Jaamadagnaya Vidmahe Mahaviraya Dheemahi, Tannah Parasuramah Prachodayat.

24. Om Dakshinamurtaye Vidmahe Dhyanasthaya Dheemahi, Tanno Dheesah Prachodayat.

25. Om Gurudevaya Vidmahe Parabrahmane Dheemahi, Tanno Guruh Prachodayat.

26. Om Hamsaya Vidmahe Paramahamsaya Dheemahi, Tanno Hamsah Prachodayat.

27. Om Paramahamsaya Vidmahe Mahatattvaya Dheemahi, Tanno Hamsah Prachodayat.

28. Om Vagisvaraya Vidmahe Hayagrivaya Dheemahi, Tanno Hamsah Prachodayat.

29. Om Paramesvaraya Vidmahe Paratattvaya Dheemahi, Tanno Brahma Prachodayat.

30. Om Vagdevyai Cha Vidmahe Kamarajaya Dheemahi, Tanno Devi Prachodayat.

31. Om Mahadevyai Cha Vidmahe Vishnupatnayi Cha Dheemahi, Tanno Lakshmih Prachodayat.

32. Om Sarvasammohinyai Vidmahe Visvajananyai Dheemahi, Tannah Saktih Prachodayat.

33. Om Bhagavatyai Cha Vidmahe Mahesvaryai Cha Dheemahi, Tanno Annapurna Prachodayat.

34. Om Kaalikayai Cha Vidmahe Smasanavasinyai Dheemahi, Tanno Aghora Prachodayat.

* * *

Anushtubha Mantra

Narasimha-Mantra

१. ॐ उग्रं वीरं महाविष्णुं ज्वलन्तं विश्वतोमुखम् ।
नृसिंहं भीषणं भद्रं मृत्युमृत्युं नमाम्यहम् ॥

Rama-Mantra

२. ॐ रामभद्र महेष्वास रघुवीर नृपोत्तम।
भो दशास्यान्तकास्माकं रक्षां कुरु श्रियं च मे॥

Krishna-Mantra

I

३. ॐ कृष्णाय वासुदेवाय हरये परमात्मने।
प्रणतक्लेशनाशाय गोविन्दाय नमो नमः॥

II

४. ॐ कृष्णाय वासुदेवाय देवकीनन्दनाय च
नन्दगोपकुमाराय गोविन्दाय नमो नमः॥

III

५. ॐ कृष्णाय यादवेन्द्राय ज्ञानमुद्राय योगिने।
नाथाय रुक्मिणीशाय नमो वेदान्तवेदिने॥

IV

६. ॐ वसुदेवसुतं देवं कंसचाणूरमर्दनम् ।
देवकीपरमानन्दं कृष्णं वन्दे जगद्गुरुम् ॥

Hayagriva-Mantra

७. ॐ ऋग्यजुःसामरूपाय वेदांहरणकर्मणे।
प्रणवोद्गीतवपुषे महाश्वशिरसे नमः॥

Transliteration

1. Om Ugram Viram Mahavishnum Jvalantam Visvatomukham, Nrisimham Bhishanam Bhadram Mrityumrityum Namamyaham.

2. Om Ramabhadra Maheshvasa Raghuvira Nripottama, Bho Dasasyantakasmakam Raksham Kuru Sriyam Cha Me.

3. Om Krishnaya Vaasudevaya Haraye Paramatmane, Pranataklesanasaya Govindaya Namo Namah.

4. Om Krishnaya Vaasudevaya Devakinandanaya Cha, Nandagopakumaraya Govindaya Namo Namah.

5. Om Krishnaya Yadavendraya Jnanamudraya Yogine, Nathaya Rukminisaya Namo Vedantavedine.

6. Om Vasudevasutam Devam Kamsachanuramardanam, Devakiparamanandam Krishnam Vande Jagadgurum.

7. Om Rigyajussamarupaya Vedaaharanakarmane, Pranavodgitavapushe, Mahasvasirase Namah.

Mantra for Self-Surrender

ॐ नमोऽस्तु ते महायोगिन् प्रपन्नमनुशाधि माम् ।
यथा त्वच्चरणाम्भोजे रतिः स्यादनपायिनी॥

"Salutations to Thee, O great Yogin! Pray, direct me that have fallen at Thy Feet, so that I may find unfailing delight in Thy Lotus-feet."

6. Glory of Mantras

A Mantra is Divinity. The Mantra and its presiding Devata are one. The Mantra itself is Devata. Mantra is divine power, Daivi Sakti, manifesting in a sound-body. Constant repetition of the Mantra with faith, devotion and purity augments the Sakti or power of the aspirant, purifies and awakens the Mantra-Chaitanya latent in the Mantra and bestows on the Sadhaka Mantra-Siddhi, illumination, freedom, peace, eternal bliss and immortality.

By constant repetition of the Mantra, the Sadhaka imbibes the virtues and powers of the Deity that presides over the Mantra. Repetition of Surya-Mantra bestows health, long life, vigour, vitality, Tejas or brilliance. It removes all diseases of the body and the diseases of the eye. No enemy can do any harm. Repetition of Aditya-Hridaya in the early morning is highly beneficial. Lord Rama conquered Ravana through the repetition of Aditya-Hridaya imparted by Agastya-Rishi.

Mantras are in the form of praise and appeal to the Deities, craving for help and mercy. Some Mantras control and command the evil spirits. Rhythmical vibrations of sound give rise to forms. Recitation of the Mantra gives rise to the formation of the particular figure of the Deity.

Repetition of Sarasvati-Mantra 'Om Sri Sarasvatyai Namah' will bestow on you wisdom and intelligence and make you a learned person. You will get inspiration and compose poems. You will become a great scholar. Repetition of 'Om Sri Mahalakshmyai Namah' will confer on you wealth and remove poverty. Ganesa-Mantra will remove any obstacle in any undertaking. It bestows wisdom on you, as also Siddhi, wealth, etc. Maha-Mrityunjaya Mantra will remove accidents, incurable diseases and calamities and bestows long life and immortality. It is a Moksha-Mantra too. Those who do Japa of this Mantra daily will enjoy good health and long life, and attain Moksha in the end. "I bow to that three-eyed Lord (Siva), who is full of sweet fragrance, who nourishes the human beings (always). May He free me from the bondage of Samsara and death, just as a ripe cucumber fruit is separated from the stalk, and may I be fixed in immortality." This is the meaning of the Maha-Mrityunjaya Mantra.

Repetition of Subrahmanya-Mantra 'Om Sri Saravanabhavaya Namah' will give you success in any undertaking and make you glorious. It will drive off evil influences and evil spirits. Repetition of Sri Hanuman-Mantra, 'Om Sri Hanumate Namah' will bestow victory and strength. Repetition of Panchadasakshara and Shodasakshara (Sri Vidya) will give you wealth, power, freedom, etc. It will give you whatever you want. You must learn this Vidya from a Guru alone.

Repetition of Gayatri or Pranava or Om Namah Sivaya, Om Namo Narayanaya, or Om Namo Bhagavate Vaasudevaya, one and a quarter lakh times, with Bhava, faith and devotion will confer on you Mantra-Siddhi.

Om, Soham, Sivoham, Aham Brahmasmi are Moksha-Mantras. They will help you to attain Self-realisation. Om Sri Ramaya Namah, Om Namo Bhagavate Vaasudevaya are Saguna Mantras which will enable you to attain Saguna-realisation first, and then Nirguna-realisation in the end.

Mantra for curing scorpion-stings and cobra-bites should be repeated on days of eclipse for getting Mantra-Siddhi quickly. You should stand in water and repeat the Mantra. This is more powerful and effective. This can be recited on ordinary days also for attaining Mantra-Siddhi.

Mantra-Siddhi for curing scorpion-stings, cobra-bites, etc., can be attained within 40 days. Repeat the Mantra with faith and devotion regularly. Have a sitting in the early morning after taking bath. Observe Brahmacharya and live on milk and fruits for 40 days or take restricted diet.

Chronic diseases can be cured by Mantras. Chanting of Mantras generates potent spiritual waves or divine vibrations. Mantras penetrate the physical and astral bodies of the patients and remove the root-causes of sufferings. They fill the cells with pure Sattva or divine energy. They destroy the microbes and vivify the cells and tissues. They are best, most potent antiseptics and germicides. They are more potent than ultra-violet rays or Rontgen rays.

Mantra-Siddhi should not be misused for the destruction of others. Those who misuse the Mantra-power for destroying others are themselves destroyed in the end.

Those who utilise the Mantra-power in curing snake-bites, scorpion-stings and chronic diseases should not accept any kind of presents or money. They must be absolutely unselfish. They should not accept even fruits or clothes. They will lose the power if they utilise the power for selfish purposes. If they are absolutely unselfish, if they serve the humanity with Sarvatma-Bhava, their power will increase through the grace of the Lord.

He who has attained Mantra-Siddhi can cure cobra-bite or scorpion-sting or any chronic disease by mere touch on the affected part. When a man is bitten by a cobra a telegram is sent to the Mantra-Siddha. The Mantra-Siddha recites the Mantra and the man who is bitten by the cobra is cured. What a grand marvel! Does this not prove the tremendous power of Mantra?

Get the Mantra-initiation from your Guru. Or pray to your Ishta Devata and start doing Japa of the particular Mantra, if you find it difficult to get a Guru.

May you all become Mantra-Yogis with Mantra-Siddhi! May you all become real benefactors of the world by becoming divine healers through Mantra-cure! May Mantra-cure-divine-healing centres be started all over the world!

7. Practical Aids to Japa

You have now a thorough knowledge of Japa Yoga and the glory of the Name. Now start real Sadhana from this minute. I have given below a number of practical hints of great use for your daily Sadhana. Note and follow them carefully.

Fixed Hours

The most effective time is early dawn (Brahmamuhurta) and dusk, when Sattva is predominant. Regularity and being systematic are very essential.

Definite Place

It is highly advantageous to sit in the same place every day. Do not change it now and then.

A Steady Pose

A comfortable Asana helps to make the mind also steady, controls Rajas and aids concentration.

Face the North or East

This exercises a subtle influence and enhances the efficacy of Japa.

A Seat

Deer-skin or Kusa-mat or a rug should be used. This helps to conserve body-electricity.

Repeat Elevated Prayer

Invoking the aids of the Ishta Devata with appropriate prayer induces proper Sattvic Bhava.

Clear Articulation

Now start the Japa pronouncing the Mantra distinctly and without mistakes.

Vigilance and Alert Attitude

This is a very important point. You will be fresh and alert when you commence. After a time the mind will unconsciously begin to wander, and drowsiness will overcome you. Keep widely alert throughout.

Japa Maala (Rosary)

Using a Maala helps alertness and acts as an incentive to carry on the Japa continuously. Resolve to finish a certain minimum number of Maalas before leaving the seat.

Variety in Japa

This is necessary to sustain interest, avoid fatigue and counteract monotony. Repeat aloud for a time, then hum the Mantra and repeat mentally sometimes.

Meditation

Side by side with Japa think of the Lord as present before you and picture His entrancing beautiful form. This practice adds tremendously to the efficacy or power of your Sadhana.

Concluding Prayer and Rest

This is important. After Japa is over, do not immediately leave the place, mix with everyone or plunge into worldly activity. Sit very quietly for about 10 minutes at least, humming some prayer, remembering the Lord or reflecting upon His Infinite Love. Then, after devout prostration, leave the place and commence your routine duties. Spiritual vibrations will be intact.

Carry on your Sadhana with perseverance and tenacity, without break, and realise the glorious Goal of Life and enjoy the Supreme Bliss.

8. Rules for Japa

1. Select any Mantra or Name of God (preferably that given by your Guru) and repeat it from 108 to 1080 times daily (one to ten Maalas).

2. Use a Rudraksha or Tulasi Maala of 108 beads.

3. Use only the middle finger and thumb of the right hand for rolling the beads. The index finger is prohibited.

4. Do not allow the Maala to hang below the navel. Keep the hand near the heart or the nose.

5. The Maala must not be visible to you or others. Cover it with a towel or kerchief, which must be pure and washed daily.

6. Do not cross the Meru (crown or head) of the Maala while rolling the beads. Turn back when you come up to it.

7. Do mental Japa for some time. If the mind wanders, take to labial Japa (whispering or muttering) for some time, or loud Japa, by rotation, and come back to mental Japa again as soon as possible.

8. Take a bath, or wash your hands, feet, face and mouth before sitting for Japa in the morning. At other times this is not absolutely necessary. Do Japa whenever you have leisure, specially during the Sandhyas or the junctions of the day (morning, noon and evening) and before going to bed.

9. Associate the Japa with rhythmic breathing or Pranayama and meditate on the form of your Deity. Keep a pic-

ture or idol of the Deity in front. Think of the meaning of the Mantra while repeating it.

10. Pronounce each letter of the Mantra correctly and distinctly. Do not repeat it too fast or too slow. Increase the speed only when the mind wanders.

11. Observe Mouna and avoid distractions, calls or engagements.

12. Face the East or the North and sit in a separate meditation-room or any good place, such as temple, river-bank, under a banyan tree or a peepal tree, etc.

13. Do not beg of God any worldly objects while doing Japa. Feel that your heart is being purified and the mind is becoming steady by the power of the Mantra with the Grace of God.

14. Keep your Guru-Mantra a secret. Never disclose it to anyone.

15. Carry on the current of Japa mentally even at other times, in whatever works you may be engaged.

9. Gayatri Mantra

ॐ भूर्भुवः स्वः तत् सवितुर्वरेण्यम् ।
भर्गो देवस्य धीमहि। धियो यो नः प्रचोदयात् ॥

ॐ . . . . . . Symbol of the Para Brahman
भूः . . . . Bhu-Loka (Physical Plane)
भुवः . . . . . . Antariksha Loka(Astral Plane)
स्वः . . . . . . Svarga-Loka (Celestial Plane)
तत् . . . . That, Transcendent, Paramatman
सवितुः . . . . . Isvara or Creator
वरेण्यम् . . . . . Fit to be Worshipped or Adored
भर्ग . . . . Remover of sins and ignorance; Glory, Effulgence
देवस्य . . . . . Resplendent (Jnana-Svarupa); Shining
धीमहि . . . . . We meditate
धियः . . . . . . Buddhis, intellects, understandings
यः . . . . Which, Who

नः . . . . Our

प्रचोदयात्. . . . Enlighten, guide, impel

"We meditate on that Isvara's Glory who has created the Universe, who is fit to be worshipped, who is the embodiment of Knowledge and Light, who is the remover of all sins and ignorance. May He enlighten our intellects."

What is that enlightenment? Now you have Deha-Atmabuddhi, a Buddhi that makes you to identify yourself with the body, to mistake the body for Soul. Now you are praying to the blessed Mother of the Vedas—Gayatri, to bestow on you a Suddha-Sattva-Buddhi which will help you to realise *"Aham Brahma Asmi"*—*"I am Brahman."* This is an Advaitic meaning of Gayatri. Advanced students of Yoga may take up this meaning: "I am That Supreme Light of lights which gives light to the Buddhi or intellect."

In the Gayatri Mantra there are 9 names, viz., 1. Om, 2. Bhuh, 3. Bhuvah, 4. Svah, 5. Tat, 6. Savituh, 7. Varenyam, 8. Bhargah and 9. Devasya. Through these nine names the Lord is praised. 'Dheemahi' signifies worship of or meditation on the Lord. 'Dhiyo Yo Nah Prachodayat' is a prayer. Herein there are five halts or stops, viz., 'Om' is the first stop; 'Bhur Bhuvah Svah' the second; 'Tat Savitur Varenyam' the third; 'Bhargo Devasya Dheemahi' the fourth; and 'Dhiyo Yo Nah Prachodayat' the fifth. While chanting and doing Japa of the Mantra, you should stop a little at every stop or halt.

Savita is the presiding Deity of the Gayatri Mantra, Fire (Agni) is the mouth, Visvamitra is the Rishi and Gayatri is the metre. This Mantra is recited during the investiture of sacred thread, practice of Pranayama and Japa, etc. What Gayatri is, the same is Sandhya, and what Sandhya is, the same is Gayatri. Sandhya and Gayatri are identical. He who meditates on Gayatri, meditates on Lord Vishnu, the Supreme Lord of the Universe.

A man can repeat the Gayatri Mantra mentally, in all states, even while lying, sitting, walking, etc. There is no sin of commission or omission of any sort in its repetition. One should thus perform Sandhya-Vandana with this Gayatri Mantra three times every day, in the morning, noon and evening. It is the

Gayatri Mantra alone that can be commonly prescribed for all the Hindus. The Lord commands in the Vedas: "Let (one) Mantra be common to all"—*"Samano Mantrah."* Hence the Gayatri should be the one Mantra for all the Hindus. "The secret lore of the Upanishads is the essence of the four Vedas, while Gayatri with the three *Vyahritis* is the essence of the Upanishads." He is the real Brahmana who knows and understands thus the Gayatri. Without its knowledge he is a Sudra, though he may be well-versed in the four Vedas.

Benefits of Gayatri Japa

Gayatri is the mother of the Vedas and is the destroyer of sins. There is nothing more purifying, on the earth as well as in the heaven, than the Gayatri. The Japa of Gayatri brings the same fruit as the recitation of all the four Vedas together with the Angas. This single Mantra repeated three times a day brings great good (Kalyana or Moksha). It is the supreme Mantra of the Vedas. It destroys all sins. It bestows splendid health, beauty, strength, vigour, vitality and magnetic aura in the face (Brahmic effulgence).

Gayatri destroys the three kinds of *Taapa* or pain. Gayatri bestows on one the four kinds of Purushartha, viz., Dharma (righteousness), Artha (wealth), Kama (desired objects) and Moksha (Liberation or freedom). It destroys the three Granthis or knots of ignorance, Avidya, Kama and Karma. Gayatri purifies the mind. Gayatri bestows on the Upasaka Ashta-Siddhis. Gayatri makes a man powerful and highly intelligent. Gayatri eventually gives Liberation or emancipation from the wheel of birth and death.

The repetition or Japa of Gayatri brings the Darsana of Gayatri and finally leads to the realisation of the Advaitic Brahman or Unity of Consciousness (Tanmayata, Talleenata, Tadrupata, Tadakarata) and the aspirant who asked for light from Gayatri, in the beginning, sings now in exuberant joy: "I am that Light of lights that gives light to the Buddhi."

May Gayatri, the Blessed Mother of the Vedas, bestow on us right understanding, pure intellect, right conduct and right thinking! May She guide us in all our actions! May She deliver us from the Samsaric wheel of birth and death! Glory! Glory unto Gayatri, the Creatress, the Generatrix of this Universe!

Glory of Gayatri

(Manu Smriti, Chapter II)

Brahma milked out, as it were, from the three Vedas, the letter A, the letter U, and the letter M, formed by their coalition the triliteral monosyllable, together with the three mysterious expressions, Bhuh, Bhuvah and Svah, or earth, sky and heaven.

From the three Vedas, again, the Lord of creatures, incomprehensibly exalted, successfully milked out the three measures (feet) of that ineffable text, beginning with the word Tat, and entitled Savitri or Gayatri.

And a twice-born man, who being away from the multitude, shall repeat 1000 times those three (i.e., OM, the Vyahritis and the Gayatri) shall be released in a month even from a great offence, as a snake from its slough.

The three great immutable words, preceded by the triliteral syllable and followed by the Gayatri which consists of three measures, must be considered as the mouth or the principal part of the Veda.

Whoever shall repeat day by day for three years without negligence, that sacred text, shall hereafter approach the divine essence, move as freely as air and assume an ethereal form.

The triliteral monosyllable is an emblem of the supreme; the suppression of breath with the mind fixed on God is the highest devotion; nothing is more exalted than the Gayatri; a declaration of truth is more excellent than silence.

All rites ordained in the Veda, oblations to fire, and solemn sacrifices pass away; but that which does not pass away, is declared to be the syllable OM, thence called Akshara Brahman. All the words should be repeated slowly without mutilation and with Akshara-Suddhi. You must not be hasty in the performance of Japa. You can make as many Purascharanas as you like, but do them slowly and steadily.

The four domestic sacraments which are accompanied with the appointed sacrifice are not equal, though all be united, to a sixteenth part of the sacrifice performed by a repetition of the Gayatri.

By the sole repetition of the Gayatri a Brahmana attains beatitude, let him perform or not perform any other religious act.

Chhandogya Upanishad

"Verily, all this creation is Gayatri. Speech is Gayatri; by speech is all this creation preserved. The Gayatri is verily composed of four feet, and possesseth six characteristics. The creations constitute the glories of Gayatri. The Brahman, i.e., the being indicated in the Gayatri, is verily the space which surroundeth man. This space is the same as the one within man" (Chap. III, Sec. XII).

"Verily, man is Yajna (sacrifice). The first twenty-four years of his life constitute the morning ritual, for the Gayatri includes 24 letters and it is the Gayatri through which the morning ritual is performed" (Chap. III, Sec. XVI).

Gayatri-Purascharana

The Brahma-Gayatri Mantra has twenty-four Aksharas. So, one Gayatri-Purascharana constitutes the repetition or Japa of Gayatri Mantra 24 lakh times. There are various rules for Purascharana. If you repeat the Mantra 3,000 times daily, you should keep up the number daily all throughout till you finish the full 24 lakhs. Cleanse the mirror of the Manas (mind) of its Mala (impurities) and prepare the ground for the sowing of the spiritual seed.

The Maharashtrians are very fond of Gayatri-Purascharana. There are in Poona and other places persons who have performed Purascharana several times. Sri Pandit Madan Mohan Malaviyaji is a votary of Gayatri-Purascharana. The success in his life and the establishment of a grand Hindu University at Banaras is all attributable to his Gayatri-Japa and the benign grace of the Blessed Mother Gayatri.

Swami Vidyaranya, the reputed author of the celebrated *Panchadasi*, performed Gayatri-Purascharana. The Mother gave him Darsana and granted him a boon. Swami Vidyaranya asked: "O Mother! There is great famine in the Deccan. Let there be a shower of gold to relieve the immense distress of the people." Accordingly, there was a shower of gold. Such is the power or Sakti of the Gayatri-Mantra.

Only Yoga-Bhrashtas and pure-minded persons can have Darsana of Gayatri by doing only one Purascharana. As the minds of the vast majority of persons in this Kali Yuga are filled with various sorts of impurities, one has to do more than one Purascharana according to the degree of impurity of the mind. The more the impurities, the greater is the number of Purascharanas. The famous Swami Madhusudana Saraswati did Seventeen Purascharanas of Krishna-Mantra. He did not get Darsana of the Lord Sri Krishna, on account of the sins committed in killing 17 Brahmins in his previous births. But he had Darsana of the Lord when he was on the half way of the eighteenth Purascharana. The same rule applies to Gayatri-Purascharana also.

Hints on Gayatri Japa

1. After the Purascharana is over perform Havan and feed Brahmins, Sadhus and poor people to propitiate the Goddess.

2. Those who wish to do Purascharana may live on milk and fruits. This makes the mind Sattvic. One will derive great spiritual benefits.

3. There are no restrictions of any kind when you repeat a Mantra with Nishkama Bhava for attaining Moksha. Restrictions or Vidhis come in only when you want to get worldly gains, when you do the Japa with Sakama Bhava.

4. When a Purascharana of Gayatri is done on the banks of the Ganga, underneath an Asvattha tree or the Panchavrikshas, Mantra-Siddhi comes in rapidly.

5. If you repeat Gayatri 4000 times daily, you can finish the Purascharana in one year, seven months and twenty-five days. If you do the Japa slowly it will lake at least 10 hours to finish 4000 daily. Anyhow, the same number should be repeated daily.

6. You must observe strict Brahmacharya when you do Purascharana. Then you can have Darsana of Gayatri easily.

7. The practice of Akhanda Mouna (unbroken silence) during Purascharana is highly beneficial. Those who are not able to practise this, can observe full Mouna for a week in a month, or only on Sundays.

8. Those who practise Purascharana should not get up from the Asana or the pose till they finish the fixed number. Also, they should not change the pose.

9. Counting can be done through Maala, fingers or watch. Count the exact number that you can do in one hour. Suppose you can repeat the Gayatri-Mantra 400 times in one hour, then Japa for ten hours means 10 X 400=4000. There is more concentration in counting the number through watch.

There are three varieties of the forms of Gayatri, for meditation in the morning, noon and evening. But many meditate on the five-faced Gayatri alone throughout the day.

Chapter Four

SADHANA

1. Need for a Guru

A Guru is necessary. The spiritual path is beset with many obstacles. The Guru will guide the aspirants safely and remove all sorts of obstacles and difficulties.

Guru, Isvara, Brahman, Truth and OM are one. Serve the Guru with intense Bhakti (Guru Seva). Please him in all possible ways. Have the mind fixed on Guru as Atman (Atma-Lakshya). Obey him implicitly. His words must be gospel truths for you. Then only you will improve. You will get His Grace. There is no other way.

You will have to deify your Guru. You must superimpose all the attributes of Isvara and Brahman on him. You must take him as an actual God incarnate. You must never look into his Doshas or defects. You should see only the Divinity in him. Then only you will realise Brahman in and through the Guru.

The physical form of the Guru will slowly vanish. You will realise the Vyapaka (all-pervading) Atman in and through him. You will see your Guru in all forms, animate and inanimate.

There is no other way for overhauling the vicious worldly Samskaras and the passionate nature of raw, worldly-minded persons than the personal contact with and service of the Guru.

An aspirant who, with great devotion, attends on his Guru in his personal services, quickly purifies his heart. This is the surest and easiest way for self-purification; I assure you boldly.

It is better if you get your Mantra from your Guru. This has a tremendous effect on the disciple. The Guru imparts his Sakti along with the Mantra. If you cannot get a Guru, you can select any Mantra according to your own liking and taste and repeat it mentally, daily, with Sraddha and Bhava. This also has a great purificatory effect. You will attain the realisation of God.

2. Meditation Room

Have a separate meditation room under lock and key. Do not allow anybody to enter the room. Burn incense there in the morning and in the evening. Keep a picture of Lord Krishna, Lord Siva or Sri Rama or Devi in the room. Place your Asana in front of the picture. When you repeat the Mantra, the powerful vibrations set up by it will be lodged in the ether of the room (Akasic records). In six months' time you will feel peace and purity in the atmosphere of the room. There will be a peculiar magnetic aura in the room. You will actually feel this if you are sincere in your practice.

Whenever your mind is much disturbed by antagonistic worldly influences, sit in the room and repeat the Name of the Lord for at least half an hour. Then immediately you will find an entire change in your mind. Practise this, and feel the soothing spiritual influence, yourself. Nothing is so great as spiritual Sadhana. You will find, as a result of this, a local Mussoorie (a hill-station) in your own house without any expense.

Repeat the Name of the Lord with devotion in your heart. You will realise God quickly. This is the easiest method in this age. There must be Niyama (rule) in Sadhana. You must systematically and regularly do this. God does not want precious presents. Many people spend millions of rupees in opening hospitals and reading houses. But they do not give their hearts. A Bhakta (devotee) should have in his heart the all-pervading Rama, though he may see outside the concrete form of Rama with bow and arrows. Rama, like OM, is all-pervading. God is Dhyana-Gamya (obtainable through meditation) and Anubhava-Gamya (can be realised by spiritual experience or direct perception or realisation). He is Japa-Gamya (obtainable through Japa).

3. Brahmamuhurta

Get up at 4 O'clock in the morning, at Brahmamuhurta, which is very favourable for spiritual contemplation, and start doing Japa. In the early morning, after slumber, the mind is calm, pure and quite refreshed. The mind is like a blank sheet of paper and comparatively free from worldly Samskaras (impressions of Vyavahara) then. It can be moulded very easily at this time. The atmosphere also is charged with more Sattva at this particular time. Wash your hands, feet and face with cold or warm water, if you find it difficult to take a bath. This will suffice. Now, start doing Japa.

4. Selection of Ishta Devata

You can select your Ishta Devata—Siva, Krishna, Rama, Vishnu, Dattatreya, Gayatri, Durga or Kaali—according to the advice of your own inclination or on consultation with a good astrologer who will select the Deity according to the nature of your planet and sign of the zodiac. Every one of us has done worship of some Devata in our previous births. The Samskaras are in the subconscious mind. So naturally, everyone of us has an inclination towards a particular Devata. If you had worshipped Lord Krishna in your previous birth, naturally you will have an inclination to Lord Krishna in this birth also.

When you are in great agony and distress you will naturally utter a certain Name of God. This will give you the clue to find out your Ishta Devata. If a scorpion has stung you severely, you may utter 'Hey Rama'; another may utter 'Hey Krishna'; while a third may utter 'Hey Narayana'; and a fourth may utter 'Hey Siva'. The calling of a particular Name is due to Purva Samskaras. If you had worshipped Rama in the previous birth, naturally you will utter 'Hey Rama' when you are stung by a scorpion, and so on.

5. Asana for Japa

Sit on Padma, Siddha, Svastika or Sukha Asana for half an hour to start with. Then gradually increase the period to three hours. In one year you can have Asana-Siddhi (perfection in posture). Any easy and comfortable posture is Asana.

Keep the head, neck and trunk in one straight line. Spread a fourfold blanket on the ground, and over this spread a piece of soft, white cloth. This will be quite enough. If you can get a good tiger-skin, complete with claws, etc., it is all the more better. A tiger-skin has got its own advantages. It generates electricity in the body quickly and does not allow leakage of electric current from the body. It is full of magnetism.

Face the East or the North while you are on the Asana. A spiritual neophyte should observe this rule. By facing the North you will be in communion with the Rishis of the Himalayas and will be mysteriously benefited by their spiritual currents.

Padmasana

Sit on your seat. Keep the left foot over the right thigh and the right foot over the left thigh. Keep the hands on the knees. Sit erect. This is Padmasana, highly suitable for Japa and Dhyana.

6. Where to Concentrate

Concentrate gently either on the lotus of the heart (Anahata-Chakra) or on the space between the two eyebrows (Ajna-Chakra). Ajna-Chakra is the seat of the mind, according to the Hatha Yogic school. The mind can be controlled easily if anyone concentrates on this Ajna-Chakra. Sit on your seat, close your eyes and begin to do Japa and meditation.

Fixing one's eyes between the eyebrows is called Bhrumadhya-Drishti. Sit on Padmasana, Siddhasana or Svastikasana, in your meditation room and practise this gaze gently from half a minute to half an hour. There must not be even the least violence in this practice. Gradually increase the period. This Yogic Kriya removes Vikshepa or tossing of mind and develops concentration. Lord Krishna prescribes this practice in Chapter V-27 of the Bhagavadgita; "Having external contacts excluded, and with gaze fixed between the eyebrows", etc. This is known as the "Frontal Gaze", because here the eyes are directed towards the frontal bone or the bone of the forehead.

Sit on your seat and fix the gaze on the tip of the nose, from half a minute to half an hour. Do this practice gently. Do not strain the eyes. Gradually increase the period. This is Nasal Gaze or Nasikagra-Drishti. You can select for yourself either the Frontal or the Nasal Gaze. Even when you pass along the road, practise this gaze. You will have wonderful concentration. The Japa can go on nicely even while you are walking.

Some students like to concentrate with open eyes, while some others with closed eyes, and again some others with half opened eyes. If you meditate with closed eyes, dust or foreign particles will not fall into your eyes. Some students whom lights and jerks trouble, prefer concentration with open eyes. Some, who meditate with closed eyes are overpowered by sleep within a short time. If beginners start concentrating with open eyes, the mind will wander to objects. Use your common-sense and adopt that method which suits you best. Overcome other obstacles by suitable intelligent methods. Remember the story of "Bruce and the Spider." Be patient and persevering. Struggle hard, and win the spiritual battle. Become a spiritual hero, and wear the spiritual laurels round your neck.

7. Three Sittings for Doing Japa

There is a special, mysterious spiritual force or wonderful magnetic power at the Sandhi or junction of time, at sunrise and sunset. The mind then will be elevated quickly and filled with Sattva. Concentration at this time will come by itself without any effort. Japa should be done at the Sandhis. Now the mind is quite calm and refreshed. You should catch the meditative wave now; meditation is more important than anything else. After this, you can take up the Asanas and Pranayama and finish up the full course by another short sitting for doing Japa and meditation. As there is always some sort of drowsiness when you start the practice, it is desirable to do some Asanas and a little Pranayama, at least for five minutes, just to drive off this drowsiness, and to make you fit for Japa and meditation.

The mind acquires one-pointedness after the practice of Pranayama. Therefore you will have to take to Japa and meditation after Pranayama is over. Pranayama, though it is concerned with the breath, gives good exercise to the various internal organs, and the whole body. It is the best form of physical exercise ever known.

If you are tired of repeating the Mantra at one stroke, have 3 or more sittings, say, in the morning from 4 O'clock to 7, in the evening from 4 to 5, and at night from 6 to 8. Repeat the Mantra very, very quickly for sometime, when you find that the mind is wandering much. The golden rule is to repeat the Mantra neither too slow nor too quick. Observe the happy medium. The

Aksharas of the Mantra should be pronounced properly. And also, the Mantra should be repeated Akshara-Laksha. If there are 5 Aksharas or letters in the Mantra it should be repeated 5 lakh times. This is Akshara-Laksha repetition.

If you sit by the side of a river, lake or well, in a temple, at the foot or top of a mountain, in a lovely garden or solitary room, the mind will be focused quite easily, without much effort. If you repeat the Mantra, when the stomach is overloaded, you will feel drowsy. Take light Sattvic food. Repeat any prayer and then sit for Japa. The mind will then be elevated. You will find it pleasant to rotate the beads easily. You must use your common-sense throughout your spiritual practice. For sometime you can visit holy places like Rishikesh, Haridwar, Varanasi, etc., and there you can do Japa on the banks of holy rivers like the Ganga. You will find marked improvement. As the mind, while in such sacred places, is free from business, worries and family-anxieties, you can have an efficient turn of Japa owing to good concentration there. Record the Japa in your spiritual diary.

Keep a diary to record the number of Japa daily. When you roll the beads do not use the index finger. Use the right thumb and the middle finger. Cover your fingers with a piece of cloth or a towel or a specially made cap. Others should not see you rolling the beads.

Introspect. Look within. Watch the mind and its Vrittis (thought-waves) carefully. Sit in a solitary room for sometime. Just as the mind wants variety in eating, it wants variety in Japa also. When it gets tired of Manasika Japa, when you notice that it has begun to wander about, take to loud repetition. The ears also will hear the Mantra. There will be more concentration now for sometime. One disadvantage in loud repetition is that you get tired of it after about an hour. You will have to combine the three methods, viz., Manasika Japa, Upamsu Japa and Vaikhari Japa to the best advantage. Use your common-sense. A beginner with a coarse and gross mind (Sthula-Buddhi) will find it difficult to do Manasika Japa to start with.

Manasika Japa of Rama-Mantra can be associated with the breath as in "Soham" Japa or Ajapa-Japa. A Japa that is done without moving the lips is Ajapa. When you inhale the air repeat mentally 'Ra'; when you exhale repeat mentally 'Ma'. Keep up the practice even during walking. For sometime, this method would appear easy. During meditation inside the room you can have this practice. This is the Ajapa way of doing Rama-Mantra-Japa.

8. Need for a Maala

You must have a rosary or Japa-Maala always in your pocket or neck and underneath your pillow at night when you go to sleep. It will remind you of God when you forget Him owing to the force of Maya or Avidya (ignorance). At night when you get up for micturition, the Maala will remind you to roll it once or twice. A Maala is a strong weapon, as it were, to annihilate the mind. It is a powerful whip to goad the mind towards God or Brahman. A Rudraksha-Maala or a Tulasi-Maala of 108 beads can be used while doing Japa.

Just as the ideas of courts, cases, documents and clients get associated with your mind when you see or think of a lawyer, just as the ideas of dispensary, patients, drugs, chemicals, diseases and hospitals get associated when you see or think of a doctor, so also the ideas of Sanctity, Purity, Divinity, Divine Glory, Divine Splendour, Divine Wisdom, Divine Power, Divine Love, Omnipotence, and all such Divine attributes get associated with the mind when you see or think of a Maala. Therefore wear the Maala always round your neck and do Japa with it. Do not feel shy to wear this, O educated persons! This will always remind you of God and God-realisation. This is more valuable than a golden necklace bedecked with nine kinds of precious stones, because this fills your mind with Divine thoughts, and is the instrument to take you to the Goal and liberate you from the Samsaric wheel of birth and death.

9. How to Use a Japa-Maala

Generally a Japa-Maala or rosary contains 108 beads. One bead among these will be slightly bigger than the rest. This is called the Meru. This is the guiding bead to indicate that you have done 108 times Japa of a particular Mantra. In doing Japa with the Maala you should note that you do not cross the Meru bead. When you come to this bead you should turn your fingers back and begin the next Maala of Japa from the last bead of the previous Maala. Thus you should turn your fingers whenever you finish a Maala of Japa, but should not cross the Meru.

While doing Japa with the Maala, the index finger (the finger next to the thumb) should not be used. The thumb and the third finger should roll the beads.

10. How to Count Japa

If you have no Maala, you can, for counting the number of Japa done, use the fingers of your right hand. The left thumb can dexterously count the number of Japa along the three lines in each finger. After you have finished one Maala of Japa put your left thumb on the first line of the little finger. Then raise it to the line above, and so on. When you finish all the lines of the five fingers it will come to 15 Maalas. You can repeat this again. Or you can use small pieces of stones for each Maala or for every 15 Maalas. Or there is another method. Mark with the help of a watch placed in front of you how much Japa you are able to do in 2 hours. If within 2 hours you are able to do 12,600 times Rama-Japa or OM-Japa, repeat thus for 2 hours on the following days also. You have now an easy ready reckoner with you. Japa of OM or Rama for a period of 2 hours means repetition of the same 12,600 times.

11. Three Varieties of Japa

Repeat the Mantra verbally for sometime, in a whisper for sometime, and mentally for sometime. The mind wants variety. It gets disgusted with any monotonous practice. The mental repetition is very powerful. It is termed Manasika Japa. The verbal repetition is called Vaikhari Japa. Repetition in a whisper or humming is termed Upamsu Japa. Even mechanical repetition of Japa without any Bhava has a great purifying effect on the heart or the mind. The feeling will come later on when the process of mental purification goes on.

The loud Japa shuts out all worldly sounds. There is no break of Japa here. This is one advantage in loud Japa. Manasika Japa is difficult for ordinary people, and break may come in the mind after a while. Whenever sleep tries to overpower you when doing Japa at night, take the Maala in your hand and roll the beads. This will put a check to sleep. This is another advantage in loud Japa. Repeat the Mantra loudly. Give up Manasika Japa at this time. The Maala will remind you of the stoppage of Japa. When sleep comes in, stand up and do the Japa.

Sandilya says in Sandilya Upanishad: "The Vaikhari Japa (loud pronunciation) gives the reward as stated in the Vedas; while the Upamsu Japa, whispering or humming, which cannot be heard by anyone, gives a reward a thousand times more than the Vaikhari; the Manasika Japa (mental Japa) gives a reward a crore times more than the Vaikhari Japa."

Do Japa in the throat or Kantha for one year. This is verbal Japa or Vaikhari Japa in a loud tone. Do it in the heart or Hridaya for two years. This is mental or Manasika Japa. Do it in the Nabhi or navel for one year. This kind of Japa is associated with the breath.

When you advance in practice, every pore in the skin, every hair on the body, will repeat the Mantra forcibly. The whole system will be charged with the powerful vibrations of the Mantra. You will be even in the Prema or Love of the Lord. You will experience muscular twitchings and will shed profuse tears of Ananda. You will be in an exalted Divine mood. You will get inspiration, revelation, ecstasy, insight, intuition and Parama-Ananda. You will compose inspiring poems. You will have various Siddhis, Divine Aisvarya, treasures of Heaven.

Repeat the Name of the Lord constantly. This will lead quite easily to the control of mind. Do it with absolute Sraddha (faith). Do it with Antarika Prema (love from the bottom of your heart) and Anuraga (intense affection). You must intensely feel for the long, painful separation from Him. Tears must flow profusely from your eyes. This is Virahagni. When you repeat His Name, remember that He is dwelling in the chambers of your heart, in the Anahata-Chakra, with conch, disc, mace and lotus in His hands, in the midst of a blazing light, dressed in yellow silken robe, with Srivatsa and Kaustubha gem on His chest.

12. Mulabandha and Kumbhaka in Japa

When you sit on the Asana for doing Japa, press the genitals (Yoni) with the left heel (if you are sitting in Siddhasana) and contract the anus (Guda), the terminal opening of the alimentary canal. This is termed Mulabandha in Hatha Yogic practice. This helps concentration. The practice prevents the Apana-Vayu from moving downwards. If you are seated in Padmasana you can do Mulabandha without pressing the genitals with the heel.

Retain the breath also as long as you can comfortably. This is Kumbhaka. This will steady the mind considerably and increase the power of concentration. You will feel an intense spiritual bliss.

When you repeat the Mantra, do it remembering the meaning of the Mantra—Rama, Siva, Krishna, Narayana—all these mean ultimately Sat-Chit-Ananda, purity, perfection, all-light, eternity and immortality.

13. Japa Plus Karma Yoga

Even when you do manual work, give your hands alone to work, but give the mind to God (do mental Japa of the Mantra), like the typist or the harmonium-player who types or plays and talks to you, or like the lady who knits clothes and talks and jokes with her comrades while she is walking along the road. You will be able to do two things at a time by practice. The manual work will become automatic, mechanical or instinctive. You will have two minds, as it were, for the time being. A portion of the mind will be in the service of the Lord, in meditation, in Japa, even while working. Repeat the Name of the Lord while at work also. Ashtavadhanis do eight things at a time. They play at cards, move the man in Chaturanga-play (chess play), dictate some passages to a third man, talk to a fourth man in order and continuation, and so on. This is a question of training the mind. Even so, you can so train the mind that you can work with the hands and also remember God at the same time. This is Karma Yoga and Bhakti Yoga combined. The Lord Krishna says:

"Tasmat Sarveshu Kaleshu Mamanusmara Yudhya Cha,
Mayyarpita-manobuddhir Mamevaishyasyasamsayam."

"Therefore at all times think of Me and fight; with mind and reason set on Me, without doubt, thou shalt come unto Me alone" (Gita, VIII-7). Though the cow grazes on the pasture, having been separated from the calf, her mind is always fixed on the calf alone. Similarly, you should fix the mind on God when you do Japa, and give your hands to work which is only worship of the Lord.

14. Likhita Japa

Write down daily in a notebook your Ishta Mantra or Guru-Mantra, for half an hour. When you write the Mantra, observe Mouna. Write the Mantra clearly in ink. On Sundays and holidays, write this for one hour. In a common place collect your friends also and let them write the Mantras. This is Likhita Japa. You can develop a wonderful power of concentration. Prescribe this to all of your family-members. Incalculable spiritual benefits are derived from Likhita Japa (Mantra-writing).

Of the various methods of Japa described in the scriptures, viz., Vaikhari, Upamsu and Manasika, etc., Likhita Japa is very efficacious. It helps the Sadhaka in concentration of the mind and gradually leads to meditation.

An aspirant should select the Mantra of his tutelary deity, or Ishta, according to his liking or inclination. Repetition of the same Mantra with meaning and Bhava should be practised both orally and in writing. For oral Japa, the help of a Maala or rosary is required. For Likhita Japa a notebook and a pen should be used. In Mantra-writing there is no restriction about any particular script. It may be written in any language. The following rules may be observed while practising Mantra-writing:—

1. Regularity and punctuality of time should be observed. This would itself bring the requisite help and be of the utmost benefit to the Sadhaka.

2. Physical and mental purity should be observed. Before sitting for Mantra-writing, the face, hands and feet should be washed. Effort should be made to keep the mind pure during Mantra-writing. Drive out all worldly thoughts while writing Mantra.

3. Continue to sit in one pose as long as possible. Frequent change of a pose or Asana should be avoided. Sitting in one Asana would increase your power of endurance and also considerable energy will be preserved.

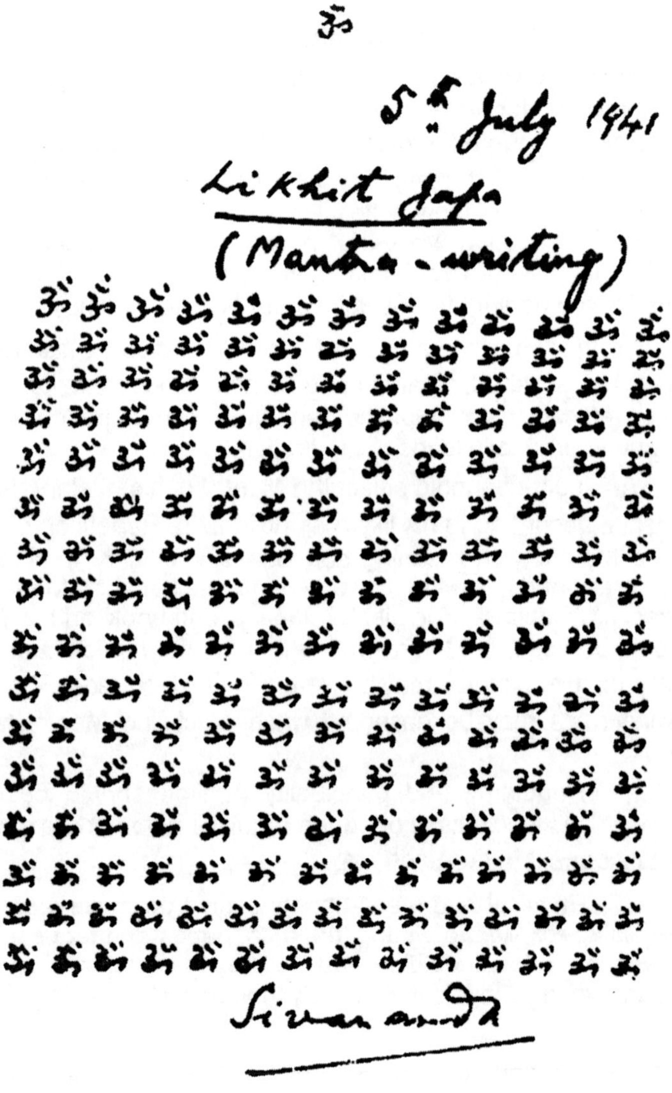
ॐ

5th July 1941

Likhit Japa

(Mantra-writing)

Sivananda

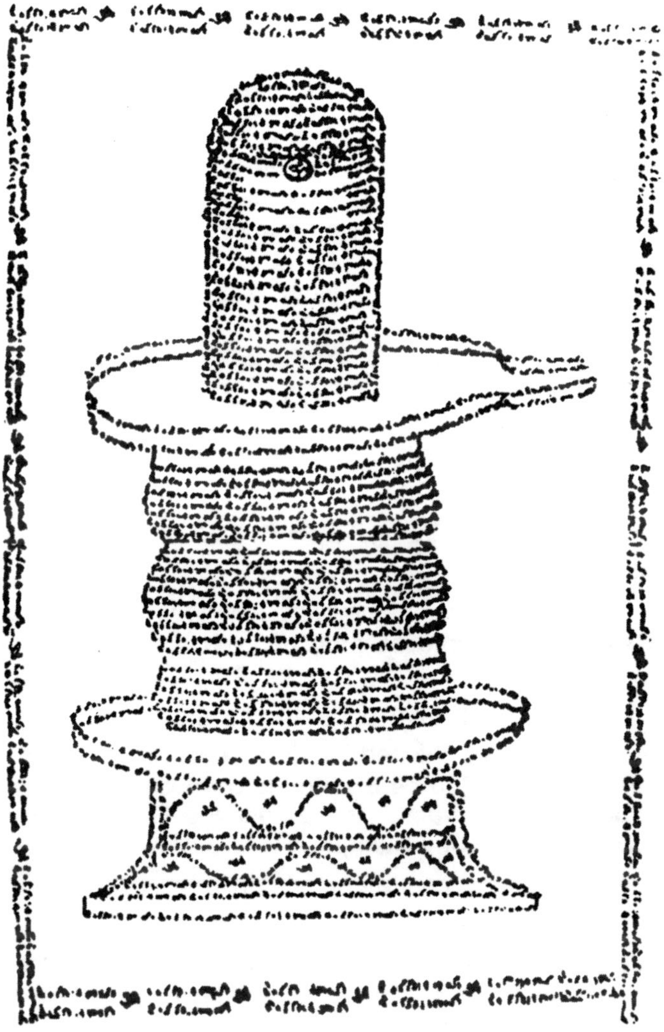

Enthusiastic devotees adopt various designs for Likhita Japa. Above is one such. Done with Bhava and Bhakti, this method achieves concentration of mind very effectively.

4. Observe silence during the practice. Too much of speaking results in waste of energy and waste of time. Silence helps in an increased outturn of work.

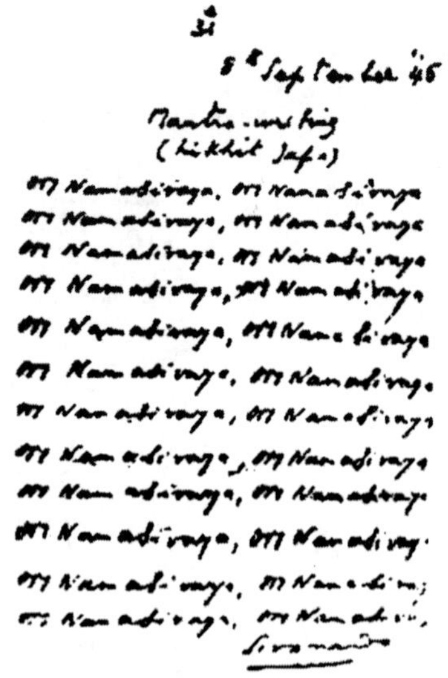

5. Avoid looking hither and thither. Fix your eyes on the notebook. This would help concentration of mind during the practice.

6. Repeat the Mantra mentally also while writing it in the notebook. This will make a threefold impression in your mind. Gradually your whole being will be involved and engrossed in the Mantra.

7. Fix a particular number of Mantras for one sitting. This will keep your practice intact and you will never get out of touch with the Mantra.

8. When you have once started the practice, do not leave it till you have finished the daily quota of one sitting. Do not allow your mind to be diverted to other engagements, as this would be an obstruction in the Sadhana. Have at least half an hour's writing at one sitting.

9. To help concentration, one uniform system of writing from top to bottom or from left to right, may be maintained during a particular sitting. The whole Mantra should be written at once in continuity. Do not break the Mantra in the middle when you come to the end of a line.

10. When a Mantra is selected by you, try to stick to it tenaciously. Frequent change of Mantra is not advisable.

The above rules if strictly observed, will help you much in your quick evolution. You will develop concentration wonderfully. By prolonged and constant practice the inherent power of the Mantra (Mantra-Sakti) will be awakened, which will fill your very existence with the Divinity of the Mantra.

The notebook should be well kept and treated with respect and purity. When completed, it should be stocked in a box and kept in your meditation room in front of the Lord's picture. The very presence of these Mantra-notebooks will create favourable vibrations requisite for your Sadhana.

The benefits of Mantra-writing or Likhita Japa cannot be adequately described. Besides bringing about purity of heart and concentration of mind, Mantra-writing gives you control of Asana, control of Indriyas, particularly the sight and the tongue, and fills you with the power of endurance. You attain peace of mind quickly. You approach nearer to God through Mantra-Sakti. These benefits can be experienced only through regular and incessant practice of Likhita Japa. Those who are not conversant with this Yoga should start the practice immediately and even if they take to this practice for half an hour daily, they will realise its benefits within six months.

15. Number of Japas

Every man is unconsciously repeating the "Soham" Mantra 21,600 times daily within 24 hours. You should repeat your Ishta Mantra at least 21,600 times daily to correspond to the 21,600 natural (Soham) breaths that every living being takes in and exhales. Then the efficacy of the Mantra is great. The mind will be purified quickly.

You must increase the number of Japa from 200 to 500 Maalas (each Maala contains 108 beads). Just as you are very keen in your taking food twice daily, tea in the morning and cocoa in the evening, etc., you must evince extreme keenness in doing Japa also 4 times, in the morning, noon, evening and night. Death may come at any moment, without a second's notice. Prepare yourself to meet it with a smile, uttering Sri Rama, Sri Rama and merging in Rama, in Eternal Bliss, Infinite Glory, Ananda and Self-knowledge. Even on your tours you must do Japa and reading of Gita. Do you not eat and drink on your tour? Do not become ungrateful to the Inner Ruler (Antaryamin) who gives you daily bread and looks after you in every way. You can do Japa even in the latrine. But do it there mentally. Ladies can do Japa mentally even during their monthly periods. There are no restrictions of any kind in Mantra-Japa for those who do it with Nishkama-Bhava, for the attainment of Moksha. Restrictions or Vidhis come only when people repeat any Mantra with Sakama-Bhava, to get fruits, such as wealth, Svarga, son, and so on. You can wear Maalas around your neck even while answering the calls of nature.

Manasika Japa takes more time than the two other kinds of Japa. But some can do Manasika Japa more quickly. The mind becomes dull after some hours. It cannot turn out the work of Japa efficiently. The speed becomes lessened. Those who calculate the number of Maalas of Japa according to the watch should take recourse to rolling beads if there be any such dullness. If there be any pain in rolling the beads you can use a 'Japa Thaili' or a bag for covering the fingers.

It is always better to take to medium speed in Japa. It is not the speed but the Bhava and mental concentration that bring about the maximum benefits through Japa. There must be Akshara-Suddhi in repetition. Every word must be pronounced very clearly. There must not be mutilation of any word. This is very, very important. Some people finish one lakh of Japa daily, within 7 hours, in a hurried manner, just as a hired carpenter or mason or contractor does the work hastily in order to get his wages in the evening. Do not have any contract work with God. There cannot be any real devotion in having any contract with God. Of course there is one advantage in doing Japa with electric speed. If the mind is dull, if the mind is wandering wildly in sensual objects, you can keep a very high speed in doing Japa, for 15 or 30 minutes. The high-speed-Japa will stimulate the dull mind and bring it back quickly to the Lakshya or the focussing point.

Those who take recourse to Purascharana and keeping up of daily spiritual diary should be very exact and accurate in keeping the record. There must be mathematical or scientific accuracy. They should watch the mind very carefully and, if it becomes dull during Japa, they should do more Japa to allow it a free margin. Immediately they should resort to Japa by Maala till dullness vanishes. It is better to take into consideration their number of Japa that is done when the mind is in full spirits and to omit that which is done when the mind is lethargic. Let whatever you do be genuine.

In 14 hours you can do 3,000 Maalas of 'Hari Om'. Japa will stimulate the dull mind and bring it back to 'Sri Rama' Mantra. In half an hour you can do 10,000 times 'Sri Rama' Japa. If you do Japa of a Mantra 13 crore times you will have Darsana of its Adi-Devata in physical form. If you are sincere and earnest you can do this within four years.

Those who wish to do Purascharana may live on milk and fruits. This makes the mind Sattvic. One will derive great spiritual benefits by living on pure Sattvic diet alone. The practice of Akhanda-Mouna (unbroken silence) during Purascharana is highly beneficial. Those who are not able to practise this, can observe full Mouna for a week in a month or only on Sundays. Those who practise Purascharana should not get up from the Asana till they finish the fixed number. They should not change the pose also. Counting can be done through Maala, fingers or watch.

The Brahma-Gayatri Mantra has twenty-four Aksharas or letters. So, one Gayatri-Purascharana constitutes the Japa of Gayatri Mantra 24 lakh times. There are various rules for Purascharana. If you repeat the Mantra 4,000 times daily, you should keep up that number daily, all throughout, till you finish the full 24 lakhs. Cleanse the mirror of the Manas of Mala (impurities) and prepare the ground for the sowing of the spiritual seed.

As Omkara or Pranava is for Sannyasins, so is Gayatri for Brahmacharis and Grihasthas (householders). The fruits that are attained by meditation on Omkara can be attained by meditation on Gayatri also. The same goal that is reached by a Paramahamsa Sannyasin, can be reached by a Brahmachari or a householder by meditating on Gayatri.

Get up at 4 a.m., at Brahmamuhurta, and start Japa and meditation. If you find this difficult, get up at least before sunrise.

It is better if you do Japa of Gayatri 3,000 to 4,000 times daily. Your heart will be rapidly purified. If you are not able to do this number of Japa, do it at least 108 times daily—36 times at sunrise, 36 times at noon, and 36 times at sunset.

16. Akhanda Japa

Akhanda Japa of any Mantra can be done. The Akhanda Japa can be conducted for 12 hours or more according to convenience. This can be done on Sundays and other holidays when more leisure is at the disposal of the members. Any number of people can take part in Akhanda Japa. Even three, four, twelve or more members can conduct Akhanda Japa. Each member should be allotted at least one hour's time. Arrangements can be made previously regarding the hour of each particular member, when he will do the Japa.

Start the Japa at 6 a.m. and continue it up to 6 p.m. One member will do Japa for one hour, say from 6 a.m. to 7 a.m. The next member is required to be present at least 5 minutes prior to his fixed time. He will wash his hands and feet, do Achamana and sit near the preceding member, take up his Maala and start repeating the Mantra in a slightly audible tone. Thus the sitting member will know that his successor has taken up the Japa, and he may get up as soon as he finishes the Maala. Keep the eyes closed while doing Japa and seat yourself in the usual pose or Asana which you are accustomed to sit on. It is not absolutely necessary that the previous member should get up immediately when his successor relieves him. He may, if he so wishes, continue the Japa as before.

The number of Maalas may be recorded against each member's name. Towards the close of the Akhanda Japa all the members can assemble together and repeat the Mantra. At 6 p.m. have Arati before the Lord's picture and afterwards distribute the sacred Prasad.

The members should not be allowed to talk and disturb others. It would be highly beneficial if, along with the Japa, the members can fast, or observe at least partial fast by taking milk and fruits. Ladies also can take part in Akhanda Japa.

Collective Japa is highly beneficial. The Mantra-Sakti is awakened quickly. The Rajasic and Tamasic forces will be soon destroyed. More Sattva and harmony will pervade the place where Akhanda Japa is done.

THE TABLE FOR JAPA

No.	Mantras	Speed per minute			No. of Japa that can be done in one hour				Time required for completion of one Purascharana, devoting 6 hours daily			
		Low	Med.	High	Low	Med.	High		Months	Days	Hours	Mins.
1.	OM	140	250	400	8400	15000	24000	Low	. .	. .	11	54
								Med.	. .	. .	6	40
								High	. .	. .	4	10
2.	Hari OM or Sri Rama	120	200	300	7200	12000	18000	Low	. .	1	3	47
								Med.	. .	. .	16	40
								High	. .	. .	11	7
3.	OM Namah Sivaya	80	120	150	4800	7200	9000	Low	. .	17	2	10
								Med.	. .	11	3	30
								High	. .	9	1	35
4.	OM Namo Narayanaya	60	80	120	3600	4800	7200	Low	1	7	0	15
								Med.	. .	27	4	45
								High	. .	18	3	15
5.	OM Namo Bhagavate Vasudevaya	40	60	90	2400	3600	5400	Low	2	23	2	0
								Med.	1	25	3	30
								High	1	7	0	15
6	Gayatri Mantra	6	8	10	360	480	600	Low	36	16	0	45
								Med.	29	8	5	30
								High	19	15	3	35
7.	Maha-Mantra or Hare Rama Mantra	8	10	15	480	600	900	Low	36	16	0	45
								Med.	29	8	5	30
								High	19	17	3	35

17. Power of Sound and Name

The power of sounds is tremendous. Ideas are generated in the mind by the mere hearing of sounds. Every name has a form corresponding to it. Sabda and Artha are inseparable. The form related to a name is at once manifested in the mind the moment that name is heard by the ears and transmitted to the mental consciousness. There are names denoting forms which are abhorred and there are also names denoting forms which are much desired. Pains and pleasures become the experiences in the mind when it is aware of hateful and delightful objects, respectively, through hearing of them. When anyone suddenly shouts: "Scorpion! scorpion!" "Snake! snake!" you at once apprehend the scorpion or the snake and jump in fright. When anyone calls you a "donkey" or an "ass" you are annoyed and you show anger. Why do you do this? Because there is created in your mind the consciousness of your supposed contact or identity with something which you think is very dangerous or far inferior to you. So you get terrified or feel that you are depreciated. That is why you jump in fear when you hear of the presence of a scorpion or a snake near you, and do not tolerate your being addressed as a donkey or an ass. Through anger you wish to show that you are not a donkey.

When such is the power of the name of an ordinary thing of this world, what a tremendous power should there be in the Name of God! God is the completion or the fullness of existence. Hence, the Name which denotes Him, too, is full and perfect. Therefore, the power of the Name of God is incalculable, for it is the height or the zenith of power. The Name of God can achieve anything. There is nothing impossible for it. It is the means to the realisation of God Himself. Even as the name of a thing in this world generates the consciousness of that thing in the mind, the Name of God generates God-consciousness in the purified mind and becomes the direct cause of the realisation of the Highest Perfection, i.e., God, Freedom and Immortality.

18. Bija-Akshara

A Bija-Akshara is a seed-letter. It is a very powerful Mantra. Every Devata has his or her own Bija-Akshara. The greatest of all Bija-Aksharas is OM or Pranava, for it is the symbol of the Para-Brahman or the Paramatman Himself. OM contains within itself all the other Bija-Aksharas. OM is the general sound or the common seed from which all the particular sounds or secondary seeds proceed. The letters of the alphabet are only emanations from OM which is the root of all sounds and letters. There is no Mantra superior to or greater than OM. OM, as pronounced ordinarily, is an outward gross form of the real subtle inaudible state of sound which is called the Amatra or the immeasurable fourth transcendental state. As the various Devatas are the aspects or forms of the One Supreme Being, so the various Bija-Aksharas or Bija-Mantras are so many aspects or forms of the Supreme Bija or Mantra, viz., OM. Even the letters `A', `U' and `M' do not really give the transcendental or original state of sound. Even this triliteral sound is only an expression or manifestation of the highest primal Dhvani or vibration. The transcendental sound of OM is heard only by Yogins and not by the ordinary ear. In the correct pronunciation of OM the sound proceeds from the navel, with a deep and harmonious vibration, and gradually manifests itself by stages at the upper part of the nostrils where the Anusvara or the Chandrabindu is sounded.

Generally a Bija-Mantra consists of a single letter. Sometimes it constitutes several syllables. For example, the Bija-Mantra 'Kam' has a single letter with the Anusvara or the Chandrabindu which forms termination of all Bija-Mantras. In the Chandrabindu, Nada and Bindu are blended together. Some Bija-Mantras are made up of compound letters, such as the Mantra 'Hreem'. The Bija-Mantras have a significant inner meaning and often do not convey any meaning on their face. Their meaning is subtle, mystic. The form of the Bija-Mantra is the form of the Devata signified by it.

The Bijas of the five Mahabhutas or great elements, i.e., of the Devatas or the presiding intelligences of the elements, viz., Ether, Air, Fire, Water and Earth, are respectively Ham, Yam, Ram, Vam and Lam. The meanings of a few Bija-Mantras are given here, to serve as examples.

Om (ॐ)

OM consists of three letters: 'A', 'U' and 'M'. It signifies the three periods of time, the three states of consciousness, the entire existence. 'A' is the waking state or Virat and Visva. 'U' is the dreaming state or Hiranyagarbha and Taijasa. 'M' is the sleeping state or Isvara and Prajna. Study the Mandukyopanishad in detail in order to understand the meaning of OM.

Haum (हौं)

In this Mantra, Ha is Siva. Au is Sadasiva. The Nada and Bindu mean that which dispels sorrow. With this Mantra Lord Siva should be worshipped

Dum (दुं)

Here Da means Durga. U means to protect. Nada means the mother of the universe. Bindu signifies action (worship or prayer). This is the Mantra of Durga.

Kreem (क्रीं)

With this Mantra Kaalika should be worshipped. Ka is Kaali. Ra is Brahman. Ee is Mahamaya. Nada is the mother of the universe. Bindu is the dispeller of sorrow.

Hreem (ह्रीं)

This is the Mantra of Mahamaya or Bhuvanesvari. Ha means Siva. Ra is Prakriti. Ee means Mahamaya. Nada is the mother of the universe. Bindu means the dispeller of sorrow.

Shreem (श्रीं)

This is the Mantra of Mahalakshmi. Sa is Mahalakshmi. Ra means wealth. Ee means satisfaction or contentment. Nada is Apara or the manifested Brahman or Isvara. Bindu means the dispeller of sorrow.

Aim (ऐं)

This is the Bija-Mantra of Sarasvati. Ai means Sarasvati. Bindu means the dispeller of sorrow.

Kleem (क्लीं)

This is the Kamabija. Ka means the Lord of desire (Kamadeva). Ka may also mean Krishna. La means Indra. Ee means contentment or satisfaction. Nada and Bindu mean that which brings happiness and sorrow.

Hoom (हूँ)

In this Mantra, Ha is Siva. U is Bhairava. Nada is the Supreme. Bindu means the dispeller of sorrow. This is the threefold Bija of Varma or armour (coat of nail).

Gam (गँ)

This is the Ganesha-Bija. Ga means Ganesha. Bindu means the dispeller of sorrow.

Glaum (ग्लौं)

This also is a Mantra of Ganesha. Ga means Ganesha. La means that which pervades. Au means lustre or brilliance. Bindu means the dispeller of sorrow.

Kshraum (क्ष्रौं)

This is the Bija of Narasimha. Ksha is Narasimha. Ra is Brahma. Au means with teeth pointing upwards. Bindu means the dispeller of sorrow.

There are, like these, many other Bija-Mantras which signify various Devatas. 'Vyaam' is the Bija of Vyasa-Mantra, 'Brim' of Brihaspati-Mantra and 'Raam' of Rama-Mantra.

Sri Vidya

Sri-Vidya is the great Mantra of Tripurasundari or Bhuvanesvari or Mahamaya. It is also called the Panchadasi or the Panchadasakshari, for it is formed of fifteen letters. In its developed form it consists of sixteen letters and is called Shodasi or the Shodasakshari. The aspirant should directly get initiation of this Mantra from a Guru, and should not start reading it for himself or doing Japa of it, of his own accord. This is a very powerful Mantra and, when it is not properly repeated, it may harm the Upasaka. So it is imperative that it should be got directly from a Guru who has got Siddhi of this Mantra.

The general rule is that this Mantra (Sri-Vidya) should be repeated after one's passing through certain stages of self-purification through other Mantras. In the beginning a Purascharana of Ganesa-Mantra should be done. Then Purascharanas of Gayatri-Mantra, Maha-Mrityunjaya-Mantra and Durga-Mantra (Vaidika or Tantrika) have to be done. After this the Panchadasakshari and the Shodasakshari have to be taken up for Japa.

The Bija-Mantras and the Sri-Vidya should not be re-peated by those who are not well acquainted with them. Only those who have a very good knowledge of the Sanskrit language and who have been directly initiated by a Guru (who has Mantra-Siddhi) can take up the Japa of Bija-Mantras and the Sri-Vidya. Others should not approach these Mantras and should do only their own Ishta-Mantras which are easy to pronounce and remember.

19. Hints on Japa-Yoga Sadhana

1. Need for Japa Sadhana

1. Man cannot live by bread alone; but he can live repeating the Name of the Lord alone.

2. A Yogi crosses the ocean of Samsara by his Chittavritti-Nirodha, controlling the modifications that arise in the mind; a Jnani by his Brahmakara-Vritti (by raising the pure thought of Infinity); and a Bhakta by doing Nama-Smarana. The Name of the Lord has a very great power. It gives eternal bliss. It bestows immortality (Amritatva). Through its power you can have direct vision of the Lord. It brings you face to face with the Supreme Being and makes you realise your oneness with the Infinite and the whole world at large. What a wonderful, magnetic, electrifying influence the Name of the Lord possesses! Feel it, my dear friends, by chanting His Name and rolling the beads. One who does not do Smarana of Hari is a Neecha (low-born). The day spent without the remembrance of His Name is a mere waste.

3. It was by the glory of Rama-Nama that the stones floated in water, and the bridge, the Sethu over the sea, was built by Sugriva and his companions, at Ramesvara. It was

Hari-Nama that cooled Prahlada, when he was thrown into a conflagration of fire.

4. Any Nama of the Lord is nectar. It is sweeter than sugar-candy. It gives immortality to the Jivas. It is the essence of the Vedas. Amrita came out, in days of yore, during the process of the churning of the ocean by the Devas and the Asuras. By churning the four Vedas, the Name of Rama, the nectar, was brought out to quench the three kinds of Taapas of the ignorant Jivas. Drink it again and again by constant repetition, just as Valmiki did in days long gone by.

5. That bungalow or palace or a place in which or where no Hari-Sankirtana or worship is done is only a burial ground, even though it is furnished with sofas, electric lights and electric fans, fine gardens, and such other things.

6. Renounce everything. Live on alms. Live in seclusion. Repeat 'Om Namo Narayanaya' fourteen crore times. This can be done within four years. Do one lakh times Japa daily. You can see Hari face to face. Can you not undergo a little suffering for a short period when you can thereby get the fruit of immortality, infinite peace and eternal happiness?

7. Japa is a very great purifier. It checks the force of the thought-current moving towards objects. It forces the mind to move towards God, towards the attainment of eternal bliss.

8. Japa eventually helps in obtaining Darsana of God. The Mantra-Chaitanya is hidden in every Mantra.

9. Japa reinforces the Sadhana-Sakti of the Sadhaka. It makes him morally and spiritually strong.

10. The vibration produced by the chanting of a Mantra corresponds to the original vibration that arose from Hiranyagarbha.

11. The rhythmical vibration produced through Japa regulates the unsteady vibrations of the five sheaths.

12. Japa changes the mind-stuff from worldliness to spirituality, from Rajas and activity to Sattva and illumination.

13. The Name of the Lord is an inexhaustible storehouse of spiritual knowledge.

14. Even mechanical repetition of a Mantra plays a great part in the evolution of the soul. Even a simple parrot-like gramophonic repetition of a Mantra, too, is beneficial. It has got its own effect.

2. Practice of the Divine Name

15. In the Satya-Yuga meditation has been prescribed as the principal form of discipline, as the minds of men were generally pure and free from distractions.

16. In the Treta-Yuga sacrifices were prescribed, as materials for the performance of Yajna were easily procurable then, and as people were slightly Rajasic.

17. In the Dvapara-Yuga worship was recommended as the principal form of Sadhana, as there was greater facility for direct worship of God, and as there was a greater manifestation of the sportive energy of God.

18. In the Kali-Yuga, as the mind of men are naturally prone to greater distractions, meditation, worship and performance of sacrifices are not possible. Therefore, loud chanting of the Divine Name or Kirtan or Namasmarana (remembrance of the Lord's Name) has been recommended as the principal Sadhana for God-realisation.

19. God's Name is your boat, Sankirtan is your raft. Cross this ocean of Samsara with this boat and raft.

20. No one obtains liberation without the Name of the Lord. Your highest duty is to repeat His Name always. Name is the greatest Treasure of treasures.

21. Rama-Nama is the true substance of the four Vedas. He who repeats 'Rama, Rama', pouring out tears of love, attains life eternal and everlasting bliss. The Name 'Rama' will guide him on the path. Therefore, say 'Rama, Rama'.

22. He who recites Sri Rama's Name can never come to grief. Lord Rama is the bestower of blessedness. He has the power to liberate people from the unceasing round of births and deaths.

23. The Name of Hari is, undoubtedly, the surest, safest and the easiest means of expiating sins. This is a well-known fact.

24. The Name of the Lord is the unfailing source of strength. In the darkest hour of your trial, only God's Name will save you.

25. Prahlada, Dhruva and Sanaka realised God through Namasmarana or remembrance of the Lord's Name.

26. The greatest of sinners can attain God-realisation through the blessings of the Name.

27. Meditate on God's Name with the belief that the Name and Named (God) are identical.

28. Japa or recitation of the Lord's Name purges the mind of all impurities and fills it with bliss. It attunes the soul with God and fills it with His presence. It brings about perfect communion of the soul with God.

29. Take refuge in the Lord with all your being, and chant His Name with devotion. This is the final verdict of the Sastras and the considerate opinion of the saints.

30. Chanting of the Lord's Name brightens the mirror of mind, burns the forest of desires and bathes the whole being in a flood of joy.

31. Resist temptation by taking refuge in the Name of the Lord. Have love for solitude and silence. Have the inward life. All miseries will terminate. You will enjoy supreme felicity.

32. Strike the chords in your heart by chanting Om, by doing Japa of Om Namah Sivaya, by singing Hare Rama, Hare Krishna; and hear the thrilling, eternal superb music of the Soul.

33. Repeat constantly 'Om Namo Bhagavate Vaasudevaya', the Dvadasa-Akshara or the twelve-lettered Mantra of Sri Krishna, the joy of Gokula, the delight of Sri Radha, the darling of Nanda, and obtain His grace and Darsana.

34. God is the one Doctor for all sicknesses. Rely on Him alone. The Names of God are the most potent, unfailing tonics, sure panaceas, well-tried elixirs, sovereign specifics.

35. My rosary is my tongue, on which I repeat God's Name.

3. The Name Is the All

36. Nama (Name of the Lord) and Nami (the Lord Himself) are one.

37. Name can bring you face to face with God.

38. Name is the way; Name is the Goal.

39. Name is a safe boat that can take you to the other shore of fearlessness, freedom and bliss immortal.

40. Name is the supreme purifier and enlightener.

41. Name is the potent dispeller of the darkness of ignorance.

42. Name is the bestower of eternal bliss, perennial joy and everlasting peace.

43. The glory and greatness of Name cannot be adequately described in words.

44. Name is filled with countless powers and potencies.

45. Name is elixir, ambrosia and divine nectar.

46. Name is more precious than the wealth of the whole world.

47. Name is the bridge that connects the devotee with God.

48. Name is the master-key that opens the door of elysian bliss and Moksha.

49. Name fills the heart with divine Prema, joy and bliss.

50. Name is your sole prop, support, refuge, solace, centre, ideal and goal.

51. Name is a potent antidote to all evils of this world. It will establish peace, good-will and unity on this earth.

52. Take refuge in the Name and constantly recite it with feeling and Bhava and single-minded devotion. All troubles, miseries, pains and sorrows will come to an end.

4. Ajapa Japa

53. Ajapa means Japa without moving the lips. It is associated with the flow of the breath. Generally 'Soham' Mantra is styled as Ajapa-Japa. The human being is unconsciously doing this Japa 21,600 times daily, within 24 hours. Will you mark the

breath now carefully? You will hear the sound 'So' when you inhale and the sound 'Ham' when you exhale. Simply note the breath every now and then, and for one hour daily sit in a closed room and do 'Soham' Dhyana—'I am He'. This is an easy method for concentration and meditation.

54. Those who have retired from service should repeat the Rama Mantra at least 50,000 times daily. They will derive immense benefit. They can do it within six hours. They will get a great deal of peace of mind, purity, strength, Ananda and Darsana of the Lord.

55. Those who have taste for music can sing the Rama Mantra, or any other Mantra. The mind gets exalted quickly. Sit alone and sing His Name. Bhava-Samadhi will ensue.

5. Bhaktas Who Realised God through Japa

56. Rogue Ratnakar became Sage Valmiki by repeating 'Mara, Mara' (the inverted form of Rama) as advised by Sage Narada.

57. Tukaram, the Maharashtra saint, had direct Darsana of Lord Krishna, several times, by repeating simply 'Vitthal', 'Vitthal' (another name for Lord Krishna), the Name of the Deity at Pandharpur.

58. Dhruva, that wonderful boy of devotion, repeated 'Om Namo Bhagavate Vaasudevaya', the Dvadasa-Akshara Mantra of Lord Krishna, and had His Darsana.

59. Prahlada uttered 'Narayana, Narayana', and saw Hari face to face.

60. Ram Das, the spiritual preceptor of Sivaji, repeated thirteen crore times Rama-Mantra; "Sri Ram, Jaya Ram, Jaya Jaya Ram", by standing in water in the Godavari, near the Takli village. He became a great saint.

61. Live alone for at least a few hours daily. Sit alone. Do not mix. Go to a lonely place. Close your eyes. Repeat the Name of the Lord silently, and mentally, too, with intense devotion. Continue this practice. You will learn to live in God. You shall have His Darsana.

20. The Glory of Mantra-Diksha

Initiation into the Divine Name or the solemn Mantra-Diksha is one of the holiest and most significant of the sacred rituals in the spiritual life. To receive the Guru-Mantra from a realised saint and Sat-Guru is the rarest of good fortune and the most precious of the divine blessings that may be bestowed upon the aspirant. The full glory of this Mantra-Diksha, specially when it is done by a realised soul, can hardly be imagined even fractionally by the initiated who has not yet a proper idea of what the Mantra and Mantra-Diksha really imply. The process of Mantra-Diksha is one of the most ancient in this sacred land and is the grandest jewel in the treasure of our peerless culture. The sacred Mantra or the Divine Name is a vital symbol of the Supreme Divinity directly revealed in the innermost depths of divine communion to the sages of Self-realisation in the hoary Vedic and Upanishadic times. These symbols are in the nature of unfailing keys to give access into the transcendental realms of Absolute Experience. Mantras are potent givers of direct experience of the highest Reality, handed down to us from those far off ancient times. Mantras have been carefully handed down to us down the centuries, generation after generation, right up to the present modern age of materialism, by the long succession of saints, through the system of Guru-Parampara.

A most tremendous transformation begins to take place in the innermost core of the conscience of the initiated or the receiver of the Mantra. The initiated is himself unaware of this fact because of the veil of ignorance or Mula-Ajnana that still covers him, even as a poor man sleeping soundly in his humble cottage at night, carried silently and deposited upon a royal couch in the Emperor's Palace, remains completely unaware of his transfer, because he is still in deep sleep. But, nevertheless, this transformation starts with initiation, and like unto a seed that is sown in the earth, ultimately culminates in the grand fruit of realisation or Atma-Jnana. To reach fruition, even as the seed has to pass through a process of developing into a seedling, a plant, a sapling and then a full-grown tree, even so the Sadhaka, after receiving initiation, must make earnest and continuous effort in the form of spiritual Sadhana if the Diksha is to become blissfully fruitful as Self-realisation. This part is the Sadhaka's sole responsibility in which task he will doubtless receive the help, guidance and grace of the Guru in the measure of his firm faith and loyalty to him. As a pearl-oyster patiently and eagerly awaits the drops of rain when the star Svati is in ascendancy, receives the drop and converts it in itself, through its own efforts and processes, into a very valuable pearl, the Sadhaka eagerly and devoutly awaits Mantra-initiation from the Guru, receives the sacred Mantra from him on the rare auspicious occasion, cherishes it and nurtures it in himself, and by his effort or process of Sadhana transforms it into a tremendous spiritual power which breaks the fort of Avidya or ignorance and opens the door to the blissful Immortal Experience.

How great a transformation and innermost purification take place from the Mantra-Diksha can be gathered from the incident in which, after the Divine Sage Narada had departed from Lord Narayana's Presence in Vaikuntha, the Lord directs Lakshmi to sprinkle water on and clean the spot occupied by Narada during his short stay. When Goddess Lakshmi enquires in astonishment the reason for this strange procedure, the Lord explained that this is because "Narada has not yet been initiated," meaning thereby that the peculiar, mysterious inner purification that is bestowed by Mantra-Diksha had not yet come to him. Such is the glory of initiation. The process of initiation links you up directly with the Divine Being. Initiation or Mantra-Diksha is at one end of this golden chain and the Lord or the Highest Transcendental Atmic Experience is at the other end of it. Now you know what initiation means.

Initiation puts you in possession with the direct means of attaining the grandest and the highest thing which can be attained, attaining which you obtain everything, knowing which you know everything, and gaining which nothing more remains to be gained! Initiation leads you to the full knowledge and experience that you are neither the mind nor the body, that you are Satchidananda Atman, full of Light and full of the Highest Bliss. May the Grace of the Sat-Guru, the visible God, bestow upon you all the highest fruit of Self-realisation.

21. Anushthana

Introductory

Anushthana is the practice of religious austerity. It is observance of certain disciplines for the sake of obtaining some object or objects of desire. The desire or the object may even be Final emancipation. Even that is a desire, though it is generally not included among desires. One who performs Anushthana has to be free from worldly engagements until the end of the Anushthana. He should be completely engrossed in one thought concerned with the austere performance of the observances prescribed by the Sastras or scriptures. Such disciplines mould men and make them fit to realise the higher objects of their desires and ambitions.

Generally the highest form of Anushthana is unselfish worship of God for the sake of self-purification and final emancipation. There is no Anushthana better than this. Other Anushthanas done for the sake of petty material ends are the outcome of ignorance and are not spiritual. Spiritual Anushthana is based on discrimination and has for its ideal the liberation of the soul from the round of births and deaths.

Anushthanas can be practised for a day, a week, a fortnight, a month, forty-eight days, ninety-six days, three months, six months or one year. The duration depends upon the ability and the liking of the performer. He can choose any kind of Anushthana according to his circumstances.

Even the rigour of the Sadhana is dependent upon the constitution and health of the individual. A sick man is not required to take cold bath thrice daily. An unhealthy man with a very weak body is not required to observe absolute fast. A person suffering from an acute disease is not required to forego taking medicine. Common-sense is the fundamental factor in all Sadhanas. No rule is an eternal rule. Rules change from place to place, from time to time and from one condition to another condition. A Sadhaka of Madras may live only with a Langoti even in the dead winter. But a Sadhaka living in the icy Gangotri cannot be expected to practise the same method even in summer. The climate of the Himalayas is not like that of Trivandrum or Madras. To hold an umbrella when it is raining heavily is not against the practice of Anushthana. The objective of all Anushthanas is rigorous mental discipline and not mere physical mortification.

A pair of shoes used when walking over the glaciers of Kailas or Manasasarovar will not prove detrimental to Anushthana. Absolute necessities of the body are not hindrances. Abnormal cravings are against Anushthana, not the normal requirements. Strict Brahmacharya is an absolute necessity for all Anushthanas. Truth-speaking and non-injury are absolute necessities; for these are mental disciplines.

Any action done against the feeling of the mind is not conducive to the rigour of the Anushthana. The actions of the mind alone are actions, not those of the body. One who feels one thing and does another thing is a Mithyachari. To him the fruit of Sadhana will not accrue. The mind is the author of all actions. The body is only the instrument. Suppressing the effect when the cause is vigorously working will not help in the annihilation of the cause. The mind has to be calmed and for that all Sadhanas are done in one way or the other.

Japa-Anushthana

An Ishta-Mantra is selected first. The object of Anushthana should be within the limits of the Mantra chosen; e.g., one should not do Japa of Hanuman in order to get a son. Foolish desires should not be cherished when performing Anushthana. One should not do Anushthana for destroying or harming other beings. This is a great blunder. This will lead to the destruction of the performer himself, in case the other party is more powerful than the performer. Generally a sublime spiritual desire should be kept in view when any Anushthana is practised.

The Japa-Sadhaka should start his Anushthana in the early morning at Brahmamuhurta on an auspicious day. He should take a bath in a river or even in the water of a well if other water is not available. He should observe Mouna all along until the completion of the day's Anushthana. The major portion of the day should be utilised for Japa. The Sadhaka should offer prayers to the sun and the Devata of the Mantra which he is going to take up in Anushthana. He should offer his daily prayers and perform Sandhya. Then he should sit on a clean place facing the east or the north with a Maala in his hand. His mind should be concentrated on the deity of the Mantra. The purpose of the Anushthana should be borne in mind all along. Complete Mouna should be observed. The eyes should be shut. The senses should be withdrawn. There should be no other thought except that of the Ideal before him.

The Sadhaka should not approach his wife at any time until the whole of the Anushthana is over for the prescribed period. There should not be any thought of wife, children or property during the performance of the Anushthana or even during rest at night. These are all hindrances in the attainment of the object desired out of the Anushthana.

It is better to feed at least one person daily until the end of the Anushthana. On the last day a Havana should be performed with Ahutis equal to one-tenth of the total number of Japa done. On the last day also poor-feeding may be conducted for the satisfaction of one's own self. Water-libations, equal in number to that done in Havana, may be given, or else (if it is found to be inconvenient) the number of Japa may be increased by that number.

To put it in a nutshell, Japa-Anushthana is performance of Japa for a protracted period with concentration of mind and without any thought of the external world. This leads to the achievement of the object of desire.

Generally as many lakhs of Japa as there are letters in the Mantra are done. But it is better to do more than this prescribed number if the actual fruit of the Japa is to be acquired. The mind of man is generally very impure and it requires much labour to purify it in order to make it fit for concentration on the Mantra and its deity. Generally many Purascharanas are required to get at the ideal in mind. One Purascharana does not bring the desired object, because the human mind is ever distracted and is filled with Rajas-and Tamas.

Svadhyaya-Anushthana

The Sadhaka takes up the study of the Vedas, the Mahabharata, the Ramayana, or the Bhagavata for reading. In the case of the Bhagavata it is called the Saptaha. In the case of the Vedas it is called Adhyayana. In the case of the other two it is called Parayana. The Anushthatri should observe the same disciplines as detailed above. Arghya (libation), Havana, etc., should be performed as in Japa-Anushthana.

Other Anushthanas

All Anushthanas can be performed on the same lines with slight changes according to the necessity of the occasion. A woman-Anushthatri will have slight changes in the rules regarding performances. She should not start the Anushthana during the time of her menses. Nor should the menses occur in the middle of the Anushthana. Generally it is better for them to take up Anushthana only for a period of less than a month. They should not suckle their children during the time of Anushthana. Even women should observe Brahmacharya during the performance of Anushthana. They also should take daily bath as in the case of men. All other rules are just like those for men. Women should not take up Anushthana of Gayatri-Japa or Veda-Adhyayana.

Generally by Anushthana the Sastras mean *only Japa and Svadhyaya.* Meditation is not considered-as an Anushthana. It is a higher step where the word Anushthana loses its meaning. Worship also can be considered as an Anushthana, though it is not included in the orthodox conception. The rules for all Anushthanas constitute the central idea that there should be exclusive occupation in the performance of Anushthana to the total detachment from all family engagements or worldly activities. Even worldly thoughts should not enter the mind of the Anushthatri. Anushthana is a great Tapas or austerity and should be performed with great reverence, faith and carefulness.

Time limit for Anushthana

There is no time limit for Anushthana. It all depends upon the liking of the individual. It can be done even for a single day. It has its own effect. But better it is to practise for long periods, since the mind is well disciplined in such practices. The longer the Anushthana, the greater the power that the Sadhaka gets. He becomes like a Yogi, possessed of health, wealth, prosperity, knowledge and power. Whatever he wishes for, he gets. Anushthana can be performed even in night-time. As a matter of fact the practice at night is more powerful and brings quicker results than the Anushthana done during day time. At night the mind is calm and free from the world. That is why all practices at night have got a greater force or Samskara.

Conclusion

Anushthana is a precursor to the practice of Yoga. It disciplines the mind and prepares the mind for Yogic meditation. It is a severe Tapascharya which if performed without any worldly desire, will lead the Sadhaka to the height of spiritual illumination.

22. Method of Mantra-Purascharana

The mode of repetition of a Mantra with feeling and in a particular manner, a definite number of times, with right observances, until a fixed number of Japa is reached, in order to obtain substantial benefit out of the Mantra, is called Purascharana.

The practitioner has to observe certain rules and regulations that have been laid down in the Sastras in regard to Purascharana and has to undergo perfect dietetic discipline also in accordance with those injunctions.

The Mantra, when it is mentally recited in this manner will bring to the Sadhaka all that he desires *within its jurisdiction.* The following is a brief description of 'Mantra-Purascharana-Vidhi'.

Diet

The practitioner of Purascharana of a Mantra should take the following diet: vegetables, fruits, milk, roots and tubers, curd, barley, Havisya (rice cooked along with ghee, sugar and milk) and which has been offered to God; or he may live on pure Bhiksha alone.

One who takes only milk-diet during the whole period of his Sadhana will have Mantra-Siddhi by repeating the Mantra only a single lakh times. But he who takes others of the prescribed diet will have Siddhi only after finishing three lakh Japas.

Place for Japa

Any holy place of pilgrimage, any place on the banks of holy rivers, caves, tops of hills and mountains, confluence of rivers, huge holy forests, below the Asvattha tree, Tulasi gardens, Devata temples, seashore, solitary places—all these are recommended as places fit for Japa. If none of these can be easily found, one may perform the Mantra-Sadhana in his own house.

But Japa done in one's house will produce only as much effect as it commonly will under ordinary circumstances. In holy places, the effect will be one hundred times more. On river-banks it will be one lakh times more. But the effect produced by Japa performed in the presence of Maha-Vishnu will be infinite.

Directions

The Sadhaka should sit facing either the East or the North, during Japa. During the night-time, he may sit facing the North only.

Bath

One should bathe three times a day, and if it is impossible, he may take bath at least twice, or even once, according to his conveniences and prevailing circumstances.

Padma, Siddha, Svastika, Sukha or Vira Asana is recommended for Japa. Cotton cloth, blanket, silk or tiger-skin should be used as seat, which will bring Saubhagya, Jnana and early Siddhi.

Japa done by sitting on Krishnajina (skin of a particular kind of deer) will give Jnana. Tiger's skin will bring the bliss of Moksha. When none of these Asanas is available Darbha-Asana, i.e., Asana made of Kusa grass, will do for the purpose.

Use of Maalas

Sphatika Maala, Tulasi Maala or Rudraksha Maala may be used for counting during Japa. The Maala should be respected and worshipped, and kept in all sacredness. After finishing Japa, it must be kept in a pure and clean place. An advanced aspirant can use any Maala, or he may not use the

Maala at all. It all depends upon the stage of evolution in which one is.

How to Do Japa

Abstracting the mind from all worldly objects, being merged in the inner meaning of the Mantra, one should repeat the Mantra, neither very quickly nor too slowly. The Mantra should be repeated as many lakhs of times as there are letters contained in the Mantra. For example, the Japa of the Panchakshara of Siva should be done five lakh times, the Ashtakhara of Narayana eight lakh times, and the Dvadasakshara of Krishna twelve lakh times. In the case of impossibility, half of the required number may be done. But in no case should it be less than a lakh.

In ancient days people's minds were very pure and powerful, and so Akshara-Laksha-Japa used to bring to them Siddhi or Sakshatkara of the Deity. In these days, however, people are of impure minds, and so they may not have Darsana of the Divinity through Akshara-Laksha-Japa done only once. Cinema-impurities, drama-impurities, and various other kinds of impurities clog the minds of the people of these days, and they are not able to achieve any tangible progress. They have to continue the Japa-Purascharana until Sakshatkara. In the case of some persons several Purascharanas may have to be done even for effecting the preliminary purification of the mind, itself. After this the Purascharana that is done will bring Sakshatkara or realisation of the Deity.

If it is found that even after the Purascharana Siddhi of the Mantra is not got, due to some old evil Samskaras of the previous birth, one should not lag behind, but perform Purascharana once again. He should continue it again and again until his mind is completely purified and ultimate Siddhi is gained. It should also be borne in mind that Japa done during the time of solar or lunar eclipse will produce a tremendous effect and hence this rare opportunity should not be missed by anybody, whenever it offers itself.

During the six seasons of the year (like Vasanta, etc.), one should perform Japa, before noon, at noon, afternoon, at midnight, in the early morning and in the evening, respectively.

Homa or Yajna

The number of Japa done during each day should be constant and should not vary day by day. Everyday after finishing the Japa, Ahutis of ghee or oblations of the Charu that are prescribed, equal in number to one-tenth of the Japa done should be offered in the sacred fire. Or else, this may also be done at the end of each lakh, according to convenience. The Havana or Homa should be performed strictly according to the rules laid down by the Brahmana portions of the Vedas, the Kalpa-Sutras and the Smritis. In this matter it is advisable to get the help of an experienced Purohita.

When the required number of Japa is over, oblations equal in number to one-tenth of the total Japa done, should be offered in Yajna, uttering the same Mantra with each offering or Ahuti.

In case one is unable to perform Homa and observe its restrictions, he can worship the Deity; do, in addition to the total Japa already done, further Japa equal in number to one-tenth thereof, and feed Brahmins and Mahatmas afterwards.

Rules to be Observed During Japa

Sleeping on the bare ground, celibacy, worship of the Deity three times a day, prayer to the Deity, faith in the Mantra, bath three times every day, abandoning of oil-bath, are to be observed strictly as vows during the Mantra-Sadhana period.

Absent-mindedness, laziness, spitting while doing Japa, anger, relaxation of legs from the Asana, speaking of foreign language (all others except Sanskrit and one's mother tongue are foreign languages), speaking with people of the opposite sex and with unspiritual persons, chewing betel leaves, sleeping during daytime, receiving gifts, attending singing and dancing, mischief-making—all these should be rigidly shunned, if one wants success in his Sadhana.

Salt, meat, pungent things, sweetmeats from bazaar, pulses, speaking lies, doing injustice, worshipping other deities, applying sandal paste to the body, wearing flowers, sexual intercourse or talking about sex-matters and mixing with such people should be put an end to completely during Mantra-Purascharana.

The Sadhaka should not sit placing one leg on the other, and he should not touch his feet with hands. Concentration of the mind on the Mantra and its meaning is very essential at all times. Japa should not be done when walking here and there or looking this side and that side. The Upasaka should never be engaged in other activities even in mind, and should not be murmuring, grumbling, etc., or covering the face with any kind of garment.

Atonement for Break of Japa

On seeing or talking with immoral persons, sneezing through the nose, passing wind through the anus, yawning, Japa should at once be stopped and is to be continued only after getting oneself purified by Achamana, Pranayama and Darsana of the Sun-God.

Conclusion

After finishing the required number of Maalas of Japa, Homa with Ahutis equal in number to one-tenth of Japa, Tarpana amounting to one-tenth of Homa, Marjana or sprinkling oneself with water by means of a blade of Kusa grass, equal to one-tenth of Tarpana, and feeding of Brahmins counting one-tenth of Marjana, are to be done regularly. The Mantra-Siddhi will then be very quickly attained.

Brightness, clearness and tranquillity of mind, contentment, dispassion towards sense-objects, will dawn on Mantra-Siddhi, if the Purascharana is done without any selfish desire or motive behind it. The Sadhaka will see effulgence everywhere and his own body will seem to be bright with light, being completely divine in nature. He will see his Deity alone everywhere and whatever he desires will be at his fingers' tips.

The aspirant, as a rule, should not do Purascharana for any petty selfish end. Sakama-Upasana will not bring to him real spiritual knowledge and experience or inner strength. Japa should be done with an aspiration to obtain the grace of God and realise God. There is nothing so great and noble as attaining God-consciousness. Therefore, let your Mantra-Purascharana be Nishkama, free from all mundane desires. Do not desire for even Svarga-Loka. Love only God and offer the Japa-Purascharana at His Feet. When He is pleased nothing remains unachieved for you. The best Purascharana is that which is done for self-purification and Atma-Sakshatkara, Brahma-Sakshatkara or realisation of God.

Chapter Five

STORIES OF JAPA-YOGINS

Introductory

Tulasidas, Ramdas, Kabir, Mirabai, Bilvamangal (Surdas), Lord Gauranga (Chaitanya Mahaprabhu), Narasi Mehta of Gujarat, and several others had realised God merely through Japa and intense devotion (Ananya-Bhakti). Why not you also, my dear friend? Why not you also become great spiritual personages? What one has done, another also can do. In this Kali Yuga, God-realisation can be had in a short period. It is the grace of the Lord. You need not do severe Tapas now. You need not stand on one leg for several years, as people did in days of yore. You can realise God through Japa, Kirtan and prayer.

I have to reiterate once more that the Japa of any Mantra has a tremendous, purifying influence on the mind. All the Saktis are in the Name of God. It makes the mind Antarmukha (introspective), turns the mind inward. It thins out all Vasanas (Vasana-Kshaya). A Vasana is a subtle desire. It is a latent desire. It is the propelling force that precedes the desire. It is a latent tendency. The Japa of a Mantra reduces the force of Sankalpa. It attenuates the mind. The mind becomes thread-like (state of Tanumanasi, the third Bhumika or state of Jnana). It fills the mind with Sattva-Guna, peace, purity and strength. It develops the will-force.

Read the book 'Garland of Letters' or 'Varnamala' by Justice Woodroffe. You will realise the efficacy of Mantras.

1. Dhruva

Uttanapada was one of the sons of the First Manu. Uttanapada means 'with uplifted foot'. This perhaps refers to the period when the Jiva, having still the spiritual element strong in him, was not fixed in the course of material descent, but had one foot towards Mahar-Loka. Uttanapada had two wives, Suruchi (with good graces) and Suniti (of good morals). Uttama or the best was the son of Suruchi. Dhruva or the fixed was the son of Suniti. Once upon a time, Dhruva found Uttama on his father's lap and wished to be there himself. For fear of Suruchi, Uttanapada did not dare stretch his hands towards Dhruva, while Suruchi herself taunted the boy for his impudent aspiration. Stung to the quick by the bitter words of his step-mother, Dhruva forthwith left the place and went straight to his mother and related to her his grievances. Suniti advised her son, who was only five years old, to do Tapas. Dhruva did not lose time but left home to do Tapas as directed by his mother. Narada met him on the way. "Thou art a child, Dhruva!" said the great Rishi. "How is it possible for thee to find out Him by Tapas, who is attainable by intense Yoga, concentration and freedom from passion, practised for several births? Desist from this attempt, my boy, for the present. Try, when thou hast enjoyed all the things of the world, and has grown old." But Dhruva was fixed in his resolve and he importuned Narada to teach him how to meditate. Narada initiated Dhruva into the mysteries of the Mantra 'Om Namo Bhagavate Vaasudevaya', told him how to meditate on Bhagavan Vaasudeva, and asked him to do Tapas at Mathura where Bhagavan permanently resides. Dhruva passed his days in austere asceticism, standing on one foot and living on air. The prince at last controlled his breath and with deep concentration saw the Divine Light in the heart. Bhagavan withdrew that Light from the heart and on the break of Samadhi, Dhruva found the same Divinity outside, standing before him. Words he had none for a time. Bhagavan, addressing him said: "O thou, Kshatriya boy! I know thy resolve. Doest thou ever prosper. I give thee a place which is ever bright and where Nirvana is constant. The planets and stars are attached to that place. Those that live for a Kalpa will die, but that place shall never be destroyed. Dharma, Agni, Kasyapa, Indra and the seven Rishis with all the luminaries of the sky, are constantly revolving round that place. Thou shall succeed thy father on the throne and reign for 36,000 years. Thy brother, Uttama shall disappear in a forest. Thy step-mother, Suruchi, shall die in pursuit of her son. The place where thou shalt finally go is my own Abode, higher than that of the Rishis and there is no return from it.

Dhruva returned to his parents and was placed by his father on the throne. Dhruva married Brahmi, the daughter of

Simsumara, and had two sons by her, Kalpa and Vatsara. He had another son Utkala by Ila. Uttama was killed by a powerful Yaksha, while out on a hunt. Dhruva went out to the North to take revenge on the Yaksha, for his brother's death. He killed several thousands of innocent Yakshas, and Kinnaras in battle. Manu took pity on them and asked his grandson to desist from fight. Dhruva bowed in obedience to Manu and so Kubera, the king of Yakshas, became much pleased with him and blessed him, too. After thirty-six thousand years, Sananda and Nanda, two companions of Vishnu, came with a chariot, and took Dhruva to the promised Abode.

2. Ajamila

Ajamila was the son of a Brahmana. He was dutiful, virtuous, modest, truthful and regular in the performance of Vedic injunctions. One day in obedience to his father he went into the forest and there collected fruits, flowers, sacrificial wood and Kusa; on returning he saw a Sudra in company with a slave girl. He tried much to subdue his passions but did not succeed. He spent the whole of his patrimony to the love of that girl. He gave up his own wife and kept company with that slave girl. He had, by her, several sons of whom the youngest was Narayana. Ajamila lost all his good qualities in low company and he forgot his daily practices. To support the woman and her children, he had recourse to all sorts of vicious and unlawful acts. Narayana was the favourite among his sons. He caressed him always. At last Ajamila's end approached. He thought, even then, of his youngest son who was playing at a distance. Three fierce-looking messengers of Yama appeared with ropes in hand. Terrified at the sight, Ajamila cried out: "Narayana, Narayana." Instantly the messengers of Vishnu appeared. At the time when the servants of Yama were drawing out the Jiva from the heart of Ajamila, the attendants of Vishnu stopped them with a strong voice. "But who are you" said they, "to interfere with the just sway of Yama?" The bright attendants of Vishnu only smiled and asked: "What is Dharma? Does your Lord Yama hold the sceptre of punishment against all who perform Karma? Is there no distinction made?"

The astral messengers replied: "The performance of Vedic injunctions is Dharma and their disregard is Adharma. This

Ajamila in his earlier days duly respected the Vedas. But in company with the slave girl he lost his Brahmanism, disregarded the Vedas and did things which a Brahmana should not do. He justly comes to Yama for punishment."

The attendants of Vishnu expressed wonder at these words: "And you are servants of him, who is called the king of Dharma, and you do not know that there is something above the Vedas, too. This Ajamila consciously or unconsciously took the Name of Narayana and that saved him from your clutches. It is the nature of fire to consume fuel, and so it is in the nature of Vishnu's Name to destroy all sins. If one unconsciously takes some powerful medicine, does it not have effect? It matters not whether Ajamila meant his youngest son or not; but he took the name of Narayana. So you must retire."

Wonder-struck, the servants of Yama left their hold over Ajamila. They went away and complained to their Master: "There must be one law and one dispenser of that law. Otherwise some will be punished and others not. Why should there be this difference? We know thee to be the sole dispenser of the Law for the vicious. But just now the attendants of Vishnu came and wrested from our hands a transgressor against the Vedas."

"True my sons," replied Yama, "there is some one above me, and it is Vishnu. His ways are mysterious. The whole Universe is in Him. His attendants always save His votaries. Only twelve of us know His Dharma, which is Bhagavata, and no one else. These twelve are Brahma, Siva, Sanatkumara, Narada, Kapila, Manu, Prahlada, Janaka, Bhishma, Bali, Suka and myself."

Ajamila heard the conversation between the messengers of Yama and of Vishnu. He became sorely penitent. He overcame his attachments, left the house and went to Haridwar. There he meditated on Vishnu, with concentrated mind. The former attendants of Vishnu appeared once more and took him on a chariot to Vishnu-Loka.

3. A Disciple

Faith Can Work Miracles

A great Guru who lived in a temple on the bank of a broad river and had many hundreds of disciples all over, once summoned all the disciples saying that he wanted to see them all before his death which was to take place soon. The most favourite disciples of the great Guru, who always lived with him grew anxious and always kept themselves close to him both day and night. For they thought that he might disclose to them at last the great secret which made him so great, and all of them fearing, lest they should miss the great opportunity, watchfully awaited the moment when the secret would be revealed. For, though their Guru taught them many sacred Mantras they acquired no powers and hence thought that the Guru still kept himself the method which made him great. Disciples from everywhere arrived every hour and waited with great expectation.

Now a humble disciple who lived far away on the opposite side of the river also came. But the river which was in high flood was too turbulent even to allow boats to pass. However, the humble disciple could not wait, as in the meanwhile the Guru may pass away. He should not tarry; but what was to be done? He knew that the Mantra which his Guru taught was all-powerful and capable of doing anything. Such was his faith. So, chanting the Mantra with faith and devotion he walked over the river. All the disciples who saw this were surprised at his powers. And recognising him as the one who came long ago to their Guru and stayed but one day and went away after being taught something by him, all the disciples thought that the Guru gave him away the secret. They sternly demanded of their Guru the reason why he deceived them thus, though they served him in every humble manner for many years, and yielded the secret to a stranger who, by the way, came there for a day, long ago.

The Guru, with a smile, waved them to be calm, and summoning the humble disciple to his presence ordered him to tell the disciples what he was taught by him long ago. The anxious group of disciples was taken aback with amazement when they heard him utter the name of 'Kudu-Kudu' with awe, veneration and devotion. "Look", said the Guru, "in it he believed, and thought that he got the clue to all. And even so is he rewarded for his faith, concentration and devotion. But you always doubted that it was not all and that something remained unrevealed still, though I told you Mantras of great powers. This distracted your concentration, and the idea of a great secret was in your mind. You were constantly thinking about the imperfection of the Mantra. This unintentional and unnoticed concentration upon the imperfection made you even imperfect."

4. The Milk-Maid and the Pandit

There was a milk-maid who was daily supplying milk to a Pandit. The Pandit was a learned man and used to deliver lectures and conduct Kathas and do preaching work. The milk-maid had to cross a small rivulet to come to the house of the Pandit. One day she came to the Pandit a little late, on account of flood in the rivulet, due to heavy rains. The Pandit questioned the milk-maid as to why she was late that day. The milk-maid said that there was flood in the rivulet and so she could not come early. The Pandit said, "Thousands have easily crossed the ocean through a single Name of God. Could you not cross this tiny stream?"

The milk-maid had great faith in the words of the Pandit. She was at once transformed. The next day when she came there was flood again. But she remembered the words of the Pandit and sincerely repeated the sacred Name with feeling and Bhava, and crossed the stream which was in floods. That day the Pandit asked her how she was able to come early in spite of the floods. The milk-maid said that she followed his advice and repeated the Lord's Name and crossed the rivulet.

The Pandit was struck with surprise. He wanted to try this method himself. But when he tried to cross the stream which was in floods, he fell into it and was on the point of drowning.

The Pandit had no faith. His was merely dry book-learning. So he was not protected. The milk-maid had true faith. So she was saved. Therefore repeat the Name of Lord with full faith and devotion. You will be ever protected by the Name of the Lord.

5. Faith: Its Import in the Bhakti Cult of Religion

Religious faith is the primordial factor in the aspirant who is inclined to follow the 'Bhakti Marga' to achieve God-realisation. One should have faith in himself, faith in his own Guru who initiates him with the appropriate Mantra, and faith in the Ishta Devata chosen by him. It is on the tripod of this faith that the fulfilment of the aspirant's object is resting.' The more the Sadhaka puts faith in his Guru in practising his teachings without the least vestige of doubt the more miraculously God's unseen force will be helping him in all his undertakings to a successful culmination. The glory of the Lord's Name and the sincere chanting or remembering of the same leads the Sadhaka towards the highest goal in life with sanguine success at every stage of progress during his Sadhana, and the utterance *"Mukam karoti vachalam pangum langhayate girim"* will actually be realised in this very birth itself.

The following illustration culled out from the great epic, the Ramayana, will amplify the above facts:

After defeating the ten-headed monster, Ravana, and redeemed Sita Devi, the Lord Rama, with Vibhishana (Ravana's brother, but an ally of Rama) and a few of the latter's followers returned to Ayodhya. The coronation over, all the invitees and other dignitaries made their way back to their respective Janapadas. Vibhishana, according to the wishes of the Lord, stayed for a few days more. Now the question cropped up as to how Vibhishana's followers were to return to Lanka in the absence of the famous bridge (Setu) which had already been dismantled. To Vibhishana the problem was very easy to be solved. He procured a dry leaf of Asvattha tree and scribbled the name of 'Sri Rama' thereon and secured the same under a knot in a piece of cloth and handed it over to one of his men and told him: "Hold fast to this knot and plunge into the ocean which will give you a safe passage through". With implicit faith, the Rakshasa, with the knot tight in his hand, jumped into the ocean; and Lo! the Divine Miracle—there was only knee-deep of water in the ocean! The Rakshasa easily waded his way to the other shore.

But when he reached the mid-ocean a sort of self-conceit and faithlessness robbed him of the Lord's benediction. He thought, "What might be in this knot of our master to work such wonders?" and instantly inquisitiveness impelled him to untie the knot and see the contents inside. The mere sight of a dry leaf itself made him laugh and scoff at it. Then when he saw the name 'Sri Rama' scribbled over it his contempt became so much that he doubted: "What? Can this name play such havoc with the ocean?" No sooner this doubt entered his mind than he found for himself a watery grave due to sudden deluge and waves of the rough sea.

The above is only one of the many instances which go to prove the efficacy of the Lord's name for the faithful and the reverse to the faithless and doubting. Let us therefore utter the Mahamantra: *"Hare Rama Hare Rama, Rama Rama Hare Hare; Hare Krishna Hare Krishna, Krishna Krishna Hare Hare"* with staunch faith and implicit belief and holding fast to the same, cross the ocean of Samsara.

Faith is the primary factor in the path of Bhakti. There is no Bhakti without faith. *"Sraddhavan labhate jnanam"*—"He who has faith attains to wisdom". *"Samsayatma vinasyati"*—"He who has doubt in his mind perishes". When the mind is fixed in a particular object, state, condition or notion with intense faith, that very thing is experienced by it. Faith is the peculiar power of the consciousness which makes one take his resort in what is denoted by it. The greatest thing in this world is faith. Without faith in the validity of experience even the dualistic reason cannot function. Man lives by faith, when faith is directed to God it becomes the cause of the liberation of the individual.

APPENDIX

1. Divine Namapathy

When allopathy, homeopathy, chromopathy, naturopathy, Ayurvedapathy and all other 'pathies' fail to cure a disease, the Divine Namapathy alone can save you. The Name of the Lord is a sovereign specific, a sheet-anchor, an infallible panacea and a cure-all for all diseases. It is an ideal or supreme 'pick-me-up' in gloom and despair, in depression and sorrow, in the daily battle of life or the struggle for existence. There is a mysterious power in the Name. There is an inscrutable Sakti in God's Name! All the divine potencies are hidden in the Lord's Name. It is the cream or the quintessence of Chyavanaprasa, Makaradhvaja, almonds, Vasantakusumakara or Svarna-Bhasma or gold oxide. It is a mysterious, ineffable, divine injection '1910194'.

You can take this medicine of Nama-Japa yourself, for curing any disease. You can administer this marvellous medicine to other patients also in your house or elsewhere. Sit by the side of the patient and repeat, with sincere devotion and faith, the Name of the Lord, like 'Hari Om', 'Sri Ram', 'Om Namah Sivaya', and sing His Names, also: *"Hare Rama Hare Rama, Rama Rama Hare Hare; Hare Krishna Hare Krishna, Krishna Krishna Hare Hare."* Pray for His mercy and grace. All maladies and agonies will come to an end. Do the treatment of Nama-Japa for at least 2 hours in the morning and evening. You will find the miraculous effect within a short time. Both the doctor and the patient should have perfect faith in the Lord's Name, His mercy and grace. The real doctor is only Lord Narayana. Lord Dhanvantari, the physician of the three worlds (who expounded the Ayurvedic Medical Science), had Himself declared: "By the medicine of the repetition of the Names Achyuta, Ananta, Govinda, all diseases are cured—this is my definite and honest declaration". In all treatments Lord Narayana is the real doctor. You find that even the world's best doctors fail to cure a dying king. You might have also heard of many instances where patients ailing from the worst type of diseases are cured miraculously, where even the ablest doctors have declared the case hopeless. This itself is clear proof that there is the Divine Hand behind all cures.

The Divine Name will eradicate the disease of birth and death and bestow on you Moksha, liberation or immortality.

The son of a landlord in Meerut was seriously ailing. Doctors announced the case to be absolutely hopeless. Then the Bhaktas took the case in their hands. They did continuous Kirtan, day and night, for seven days, around the bed of the patient. The patient stood up and began to sing God's Name on the seventh clay. He recovered completely. Such is the miraculous power of Sankirtan.

2. Nama-Aparadhas

(Offences Against the Divine Name)

It is true that the utterance of the Divine Name can absolve one from all sins and enable one to attain salvation or love of God (both of which are so difficult to get); but that is possible only when the Name is uttered with faith and reverence and the practice is free from all taints of sin against the Name, viz., the following ten offences;

1. Vilification of saints and devotees.
2. Differentiation among (Divine) Names.
3. Irreverence towards preceptor (Guru).
4. Speaking lightly of the scriptures.
5. Treating the glory of Name as nothing but exaggerated praise.
6. Commission of sins under the cover of Name.
7. Ranking the Name with other virtues and practising fasting, charity, sacrifices, etc., thinking that the Name by itself is insufficient.
8. Recommending the practice of Name to irreverent and ungodly persons who are not prepared to hear such advice.
9. Want of love for the Name even after hearing its glory.

10. Emphasis of 'I' and 'mine' and attachment to objects of enjoyment.

If through inadvertence one lapses into any of the above ten sins, the only way to be absolved from it is to repeat the Name again and repent for the mistake.

The Name itself is the best atonement for sins committed against the Name. Through constant Kirtan or Japa of the Name all the desires can be fulfilled and Moksha attained ultimately.

3. God's Name Is All-Powerful

Lord Rama took birth in the house of Dasaratha, as his son. To remove the afflictions of His devotees the Lord underwent lots of difficulties. He destroyed the suffering of His devotees and filled them with joy and bliss. But those who repeat His Names are freed from all afflictions. They attain to the highest happiness and bliss. They become, as it were, the houses of joy and bliss.

Lord Rama saved Ahalya and bestowed on her immortality by her mere touch of His Sacred Feet. But His Names have saved countless wicked men of perverted intellects. For blessing Visvamitra Sri Rama killed the daughter of Suketu, Tadaka by name. But His Name has, for the welfare of its devotees, destroyed their countless evil desires, just as the sun destroys darkness. Lord Rama, by His own effort, broke the bow of Lord Siva. But the glory of the Name is such that it destroys all fears of Samsara. Lord Rama purified one Dandaka forest. But the Name has purified innumerable minds, of their impurities. Lord Rama killed the host of demons but the Name destroys all the sins of the Kali-Yuga (iron age). Lord Rama saved and blessed Sabari, Jatayu, etc., whereas Rama Nama has saved countless men filled with the afflictions of Kali Yuga. Rama protected and gave shelter to Sugriva and Vibhishana, but the Name has saved countless poor people. The glory of Rama is clearly seen in the Vedas and is sung by all great men.

Lord Rama collected the monkeys and got ready a big army to bridge the ocean. He underwent a lot of suffering. But by the mere repetition of His Name, the ocean of Samsara is dried up. Rama killed, in battle, Ravana and his followers. Then he returned to Ayodhya, with Sita. He was then crowned as the emperor of Ayodhya. But devotees by the mere repetition of His Name destroy the mighty army of ignorance. They are immersed in the ocean of bliss. They go care-free. This is due to the power of the Name.

Rama-Nama—Our Only Saviour in Kali Yuga

Name is the bestower of powers, Siddhis, Riddhis, etc., on those who are able to bless others, viz., gods and saints. Lord Siva, realised the glory of Rama-Nama, has selected it out of crores of stories sung in praise of the Lord. He is full of auspiciousness though His Form is outwardly fearful and inauspicious. Suka, Sanaka and other perfected sages, endowed with great powers of Yoga, enjoy Brahmananda (the bliss of the Supreme) only by the power of Nama. Sage Narada knows well the glory of the Name. Hari is the beloved of the entire creation. To Hari, Hara (Siva) is dear. Narada is dear to both Hari and Hara. By the repetition of the Name, Prahlada became the dearest of devotees of the Lord. Dhruva, out of extreme sorrow and remorse, took to the repetition of the Lord's Name. Within six months' time he attained to an enviable position in the world, among the devotees of the Lord. Sri Hanuman repeated with intense devotion the Name of the Lord and became the pet of the Lord. Ajamila, Gajendra, Ganika, etc., attained Moksha by the efficacy of the Divine Name. It will swell to pages after pages to give a succinct account of all the devotees who attained to excellence by the repetition of the Name of the Lord. In the Kali-Yuga God's Name is the wish-yielding Kalpataru, and in the Name exists all auspiciousness. By repeating the Name of the Lord, Sri Tulasidas himself attained to the highest eminence. He became the pet of the Lord. Ramacharitamanas is itself the glory of Rama Nama.

Not only in the Kali-Yuga but in all ages, at all times, in all the worlds, by the repetition of the Name of the Lord, men have crossed the ocean of Samsara and attained to the highest eminence. In Kali-Yuga Nama-Japa is particularly suited for one's emancipation, just as meditation, performance of sacrifices and worship of the Lord were suited in the other three Yugas, for the attainment of Moksha. In this most troublesome Kali-Yuga there is no other Sadhana for emancipation. Rama

Nama is the bestower of bliss and immortality. Here in this world it is like unto one's own parents. A devotee of Rama ends his cycle of birth and death here itself He takes no more births. Those who have intense faith realise the infallible fruits of Rama Nama and lead a happy, peaceful life here and attain immortality hereafter. May Lord Rama bless all!

Om Sri Rama Jaya Rama Jaya Jaya Rama

4. Essence of Japa Yoga

Japa Yoga is the easy path
To attain God-consciousness;
Japa is repetition of a Mantra
Or Name of the Lord.

There should be Bhava or feeling
When you repeat the Mantra;
The Bhava will come by itself.
Do not bother in the beginning.

There are three kinds of Japa:
Mental, semi-verbal and vocal;
Mental Japa is more powerful.
When the mind wanders,
Repeat the Mantra loudly.

Sit in Padma or Siddha Asana,
Roll the beads, with closed eyes;
Loud repetition shuts out sounds.
Do alternately silent and loud Japa.

Hari Om, Sri Ram, Sitaram,
Om Namo Bhagavate Vaasudevaya,
Om Namo Narayanaya, Om Namah Sivaya,
Gayatri, Om and Soham,
Are all very good Mantras.

Select any Mantra you like,
Or get it from your Satguru;
Repeat it regularly 21600 times.
Have faith in the Name.

You can do Japa with the breath.
This will be Ajapa-Japa of Soham;
Repeat mentally 'So' with inhalation,
And 'ham' with exhalation.

You can do Ajapa-Japa of Om,
Rama or any Name;
Split it into two;
Take 'O' or 'Ra' with inhalation;
'M' or 'Ma' with exhalation.

Name purifies the heart,
Name destroys Vasanas,
Name burns all sins,
Name gives you Moksha,
Name confers prosperity,
Name removes troubles.

Do Japa in Brahmamuhurta.
Brahmamuhurta is 4.00 a.m.
You will derive immense benefits,
If you practise at this hour.

Do not bother about bath.
A bath is good;
If you cannot take a bath,
Wash your face, feet and hands
And sit for Japa and meditation.

As soon as you wake up,
Sit for Japa and meditation.
Practise Asana, Pranayama, later on.
Do not spend half an hour in cleaning the teeth;
Brahmamuhurta may pass away quickly.

If sleep overpowers you,
Stand up and do the Japa;
Or repeat it loudly.
Dash cold water on the face.

Or do Kirtan for ten minutes,
Or practise Pranayama and Asana,
Or stroll for a while, singing the Name
Or sit on Vajra-Asana.

If you finish your food at 7 p.m.,
If you take milk and fruits at night,
If you avoid taking rice at night,
Sleep will not trouble you.

You can do Japa with Dhyana also;
This will be Japa-Sahita-Dhyana.
Meditate on the form of the Lord,
When you do Japa of a Mantra.
This is more beneficial.

You are roasted in the fire of Samsara;
The only remedy is Japa;
The only refuge is the Name of the Lord.
Can anyone live without the Name?

O man, why do you waste your time in gossip?
You will have to repent in old age;
You will have to weep at the hour of death.
Have a rich crop of Japa now.

Do not argue, do not doubt.
Have full reverence and faith in Name.
Name is nectar, Name is your prop.
Cross this Samsara, with this Name.

Ramadas, Tukaram and Narasi Mehta,
Jnana Dev, Nama Dev and Damaji,
Practised Japa and attained God-realisation.
Why not you also, O beloved Govind!

Name is an asset for you,
Name is real wealth for you.
If you repeat the Name one lakh times,
You will have immense spiritual wealth,
In the spiritual Bank of the Lord.

Glory to the Name; Glory to Japa!
Glory to God; Glory to Guru!
Glory to those who stick to the Name,
Who repeat daily the Name.

Song of the Glory of Name

Sita Ram, Sita Ram, Sita Ram Bol,
Radhe Shyam, Radhe Shyam, Radhe Shyam Bol.

1. Nam Prabhu kaa, hai sukhakari,
   Pap katenge, chhin me bhari,
   Pap ki Gathari de tu khol....... (Sita Ram...)
2. Prabhu ka Nam Ahalya tari,
   Bhakta Bheelni ho gai pyari,
   Nam ki mahima hai anmol........ (Sita Ram...)
3. Sua padhavat, Ganika tari,
   Bade bade nishachar samhari,
   Jin jin papi tare tol............ (Sita Ram...)
4. Jo jo sharan pade, prabhu tare,
   Bhavasagar se, par utare,
   Bande tera kya lagta mol.......... (Sita Ram...)
5. Ram bhajan bina, mukti na hove,
   Moti sa janma tu, vyartha khove,
   Rama Rasamrita pee le ghol........ (Sita Ram...)
6. Chakradhari bhaj Har Govindam,
   Muktidayaka Paramanandam,
   Hardam Krishna taraju tol .... (Sita Ram...)

Translation

1. Name of the Lord gives immense bliss,
   All great sins in a moment vanish,
   Untie the bundle of your sins.
2. Name of Prabhu liberated Ahalya,
   Bheelni became dear by devotion,
   Invaluable is glory of Name.
3. Ganika was liberated by the teaching of the parrot,
   The great Rakshasas were slain one and all,
   All sinners were freed, being counted and weighed.
4. All who surrendered to Him were freed,
   And taken across the ocean of Samsara,
   It costs you nothing to repeat His Name.
5. Moksha cannot be had without Bhajan of Rama,
   Why are you wasting this pearl-like life, in vain?
   Drink deep the nectar of Rama Nama.

6. Always remember Hari, the disc-bearer,
   Absolute Bliss that gives liberation,
   Ever weigh the scales of Krishna's Name.

5. Questions and Answers

Question: What is the difference between Japa and Dhyana?

Answer: Japa is the repetition of the Mantra of a Devata. Dhyana is meditation on His or Her form and attributes. It is the keeping up of a continuous flow of one idea of God.

Q: What is Japa-Sahita-Dhyana and Japa-Rahita-Dhyana?

A: The aspirant is repeating the Mantra and at the same time he is meditating on the form of his Ishta-Devata. A Krishna-Bhakta repeats the Mantra 'Om Namo Bhagavate Vaasudevaya' and at the same time he visualises the picture of the Lord, Sri Krishna. This is Japa-Sahita-Dhyana. In Japa-Rahita-Dhyana the devotee continues his Japa for some time along with the meditation and afterwards the Japa drops by itself and he is established in meditation only.

Q: Can Japa alone give Moksha?

A: Yes, there is a mysterious power in the Mantra, and this Mantra-Sakti brings meditation and Samadhi, and brings the devotee face to face with God.

Q: Should an advanced aspirant use a rosary?

A: It is not necessary for an advanced aspirant. But when sleep overpowers him he can take to rolling of the beads, and when the mind is tired of Japa, by way of relaxation he can take to rolling of the beads.

Q: What is the use of repeating the Mantra again and again?

A: It gives force. It intensifies the spiritual Samskaras.

Q: Can I repeat two or three Mantras?

A: It is better to stick to one Mantra alone. If you are a devotee of the Lord Krishna try to see Him alone in Rama, Siva, Durga, Gayatri, etc., also. All are forms of the one God or

Ishvara. Worship of Krishna is worship of Rama and Devi also, and vice versa.

Q: How to use the rosary?

A: You must not use the index finger while rolling the beads. You must use the thumb and the middle or the third finger. When counting of one Maala is over, revert it and come back again. Do not cross the Meru. Cover your hand with a towel, so that the Maala may not be visible.

Q: Can I do Japa while waking?

A: Yes; you can do it mentally. There is no restriction for Japa when it is done with Nishkama-Bhava, i.e., for the sake of realising God alone.

Q: What should be the Bhava while repeating the Mantra?

A: You can take your Ishta-Devata as your Master or Guru or Father or Friend or Beloved. You can have any Bhava which suits you best.

Q: After how many Purascharanas can I realise God?

A: It is not the number of Japa but purity, concentration, Bhava and feeling and one-pointedness of mind that help the aspirant in the attainment of God-consciousness. You should not do Japa in a hurried manner, as a contractor tries to finish off work in a hurried way. You must do it with Bhava, purity, one-pointedness of mind and single-minded devotion.

Q: How does Japa burn the old vicious Samskaras?

A: Just as fire has got the property of burning, so also the Names of the Lord have got the property of burning the sins and the old vicious Samskaras.

Q: Can we control the Indriyas by Japa?

A: Yes, Japa fills the mind with Sattva. It destroys the Rajas and the outgoing tendencies of the mind and the Indriyas. Gradually the Indriyas are withdrawn and controlled.

Q: Can a Grihasta do the Japa of Suddha-Pranava?

A: Yes; if he is equipped with the fourfold discipline or Sadhana-Chatushtaya, if he is free from Mala and Vikshepa, and if he has got a strong inclination to Jnana-Yoga-Sadhana, he can repeat Om.

Q: While doing Japa of Om, does it mean that I should become one with that sound, by its constant repetition?

A: When you meditate on Om or repeat Om mentally you should entertain the Bhava or feeling: "I am the all-pervading, pure, Sat-Chit-Ananda Atman". You need not be one with sound. What is wanted is feeling with the meaning "I am Brahman."

Q: What is the meaning of the Mantra: "Om Namo Bhagavate Vaasudevaya?"

A: The meaning is "Prostration to the Lord Krishna." Vaasudeva means also: "All-pervading Intelligence."

Q: How to dwell on the form of the Lord Krishna as well as on the Divine attributes?

A: First practise with open eyes Trataka on the picture. Place it in front of you. Then close the eyes and visualise the picture. Then meditate on the attributes of the Lord, such as Omnipotence, Omniscience, Omnipresence, Purity, Perfection, etc.

Q: I am not able to repeat the Mantra mentally. I have to open the lips. Mental repetition of the Mantra takes for me much time and even the letters are not clearly repeated. Kindly tell me what is this due to. While doing Japa and meditation at a time, I am not able to fix or concentrate the mind on the Lord. If I fix the mind on the Lord I forget to repeat the Mantra and roll the beads. When I turn my mind to roll the beads, I cannot concentrate on the Lord.

A: You will have to first start with loud repetition of the Mantra and then practise Upamsu-Japa (in a whisper). Only after practice of Upamsu-Japa for at least three months, you will be in a position to do mental Japa. Mental Japa is more difficult. Only when all other thoughts subside there will be pleasure in mental Japa. Otherwise your mind will be brooding over sensual objects only and you will not be able to do mental Japa.

You cannot do mental Japa and mental visualisation of the Lord's form side by side. You will have to gaze at the picture of the Lord and mentally repeat the Mantra. Rolling the beads is only an auxiliary to concentration for beginners. The Maala also goads the mind to God. It reminds you to do Japa. When you are well established in mental Japa, rolling the beads is not necessary. Till that time you will have to roll the beads and concentrate on the picture of the Lord. You need not mentally visualise them.

Mental Japa prepares the mind for meditation on the Lord. When you are able to meditate on the form of the Lord, without fear of interruption by other thoughts, you can do so as long as you can. But the moment you are assailed by other worldly thoughts once again take to mental Japa. Meditation comes only as a result of long and sustained rigorous practice for a number of years. Much patience is needed. Beginners get disheartened if they are not able to meditate after a few days' practice.

Q: If we do Japa of a Mantra without understanding its meaning or in a hurry, will it have any bad reaction on the person who does?

A: It cannot have any bad reaction but the spiritual progress will be slow when the Mantra is repeated in a hurry-burry without Bhava or faith. Even when any Mantra is repeated unconsciously or hurriedly without Bhava, without understanding its meaning, it undoubtedly produces beneficial results, just as fire burns inflammable objects when they are brought near.

Q: What are the signs that indicate that the Mantra is really benefiting the Sadhaka?

A: The Sadhaka who practises Mantra-Yoga will feel the Presence of the Lord at all times. He will feel the Divine Ecstasy and holy thrill in the heart. He will possess all Divine qualities. He will have a pure mind and a pure heart. He will feel horripilation. He will shed tears of Prema. He will have holy communion with the Lord.

Q: May I know if mental Japa is more powerful than the practice of chanting of a Mantra loudly?

A: Mental Japa is indeed more powerful. When mental Japa is successfully practised all worldly extraneous thoughts drop off quickly. In Vaikhari and Upamsu-Japa, there is scope for the mind to have its own ways. The tongue may be repeating the Mantra but the mind may be busy with other thoughts. Mental Japa closes the avenues, though worldly thoughts may try to enter the mind. In other words, the trap-door through which thoughts enter the mental factory is closed when the Mantra is being repeated. The mind is filled with the power of the Mantra. But you should be vigilant and prevent sleep from overpowering the mind. Desires, sleep and various sensual thoughts obstruct the successful performance of mental Japa. Regular practice, sincere attempt, sleepless vigilance and earnestness can bring complete success in mental Japa.

Q: Do I hold enough capacity to be enlightened by a Mantra?

A: Yes. Have perfect unshakable faith in the efficiency of a Mantra. A Mantra is filled with countless divine potencies. Repeat it constantly. You will be endowed with capacity, inner spiritual strength and will-power. The Mantra-Chaitanya will be awakened by constant repetition. You will get illumination.

Q: What is the meaning of feeling (Bhava) when one does Japa of a Mantra?

A: He who repeats a Mantra should entertain either the Dasya-Bhava (attitude of a servant) or Sishya-Bhava (attitude of a disciple) or Putra-Bhava (attitude of a son) while doing Japa. He can also have the feeling of a friend, an offspring or of a husband in regard to the Lord.

He should have also the feeling or mental attitude that the Lord is seated in his heart, that Sattva or purity is flowing to him from the Lord, that the Mantra purifies his heart, destroys desires, cravings and evil thoughts, when he does Japa.

6. Glory of God's Name

(Gleanings)

Goswami Tulasidas has left nothing unsaid about the Glory of Divine Name. There is not the least doubt that all sacred formulae such as the Dvadasakshara (consisting of twelve letters) and Ashtakshara (consisting of eight letters) Mantras bring solace to those entangled in the meshes of worldly attachment. Let every individual depend on the Mantra which may have given him peace. For those, however, who have known no peace, and who are in search of it, the Name of Rama can certainly work wonders. God is said to possess a thousand Names; it means His Names are infinite; His glory is infinite. That is how God transcends both His Names and Glory. The support of the Name, however, is absolutely necessary for people so long as they are tied to their bodies. In the present age even ignorant and unlettered people can take shelter under the monosyllabic Mantra. When pronounced, the word 'Rama' makes a single sound, and truly speaking, there is no difference between the sacred syllable 'Om' and the word 'Rama'.

The glory of the Divine Name cannot be established through reasoning and intellect. It can be experienced only through reverence and faith. —*Sri Mahatma Gandhi*

Once you have developed a taste and reverence for the Divine Name, you no longer require to exercise your faculty of reasoning or undertake any other form of spiritual discipline. All one's doubts are dispelled through the Name; the heart is also purified through the Name; nay, God Himself is realised through the Name.

Take the Name of Hari every morning and evening, clapping your hands with the rhythm of the sound; all your sins and afflictions will disappear. The forces of ignorance working in your heart will be driven away as soon as you utter the Name of Hari with the clapping of hands.

The Name of God uttered consciously, unconsciously, or even through mistake, will surely bring its own reward. A person who deliberately goes to bathe in a river is in no way better than his friend who is pushed into the river by some one else, so far as ablution as such is concerned; and a third man who remains lying on his cot and on whom a bucket of water is thrown, also, has his body washed.

A plunge taken in a pool of nectar in any way makes one immortal. This will happen both in the case of the person who takes the plunge after much adoration and the person who, though unwilling, is forcibly pushed into the pool. God's Name uttered consciously, unconsciously, or even through mistake is bound to produce its effects.

Formerly people used to have simple cases of fever which were cured by a decoction of ordinary ingredients, but now as malarial fever is the order of the day the remedy also is strong. In days of yore people used to perform sacrificial rites, Yogic practice and austere penances, but in this age of Kali, life depends on food, and the mind of man is feeble. All sorts of worldly ills are, therefore, cured by merely chanting the Name of Hari with one-pointed attention.

—Sri Ramakrishna Paramahamsa

Blessed be the pious soul who drinks uninterruptedly the nectar of Sri Rama's Name which has been churned out of the ocean of the Vedas, which removes the impurities of the iron age, which lives constantly on the tongue of Lord Siva, which is a sovereign remedy of unfailing specific to cure the disease of worldly existence, and is life itself to mother Janaki.

The Name is even superior to the Lord, because the Nirguna and Saguna aspects of Brahman are tasted and realised by the power of the Name. Rama delivered a single lady, Ahalya, whereas the Name has purified crores of wicked men. Rama gave salvation to two of his faithful servants—Sabari and Jatayu, but the Name has been the saviour of countless wicked persons. Live on milk for six months in Chitrakuta, and repeat Rama-Nama incessantly with one-pointed mind and unshakable faith. You will get Darsana of Lord Rama, liberation, Siddhis and all auspicious blessings from the Lord.

Blessed is the son and blessed are his parents who remember Sri Rama in whatsoever way it may be. Blessed is the outcaste or Chandala who repeats the Name of Rama day and night. What is the use of high birth to one who does not repeat Rama-Nama? The highest peaks of mountains give shelter only to snakes. Blessed are the sugar-cane, the corn and betel leaves that flourish in the plains and give delight to all.

The two sweet and fascinating letters RA and MA are like the two eyes of the alphabet and the very life-breath of the devotees. They are easy to remember and delightful to all. They are beneficial in this world and sustain us in the other world.

Victory to Rama-Nama which blesses us for ever! Glory to Rama-Nama which confers immortality, eternal peace and infinite bliss on those who repeat it!

—Sri Tulasi Das.

"Oh, how amazing is the perversity of misguided people (inhabiting this globe) that they do not remember the Name of Sri Rama, which has the power to liberate them (from the unceasing round of births and deaths)! The utterance of this Name does not involve any exertion, it rings supremely melodious to the ear. Even then, misguided people do not take its remembrance. What a pity! Mukti (freedom from birth and death) which is exceedingly difficult for us, mortal men, to attain, is easily obtained through the utterance of the Name of Sri Rama. Is there anything more important for a man to do than to repeat this Name? O chief among the twice-born, Jaimini! the person repeating the Name of Sri Rama at the time of death attains salvation, even if he is the worst sinner. O chief among the Brahmanas, the Name of Sri Rama wards off all evils, fulfils all desires and bestows salvation; all men possessing wisdom should, therefore, constantly remember this Name. Verily, I say unto thee, O Brahmana! the moment that passes without the remembrance of the Name of Sri Rama goes in vain. Sages who know the Truth declare only that tongue to possess the sense of taste which relishes the flavour of the nectarine Name of Sri Rama. I declare solemnly, again and again, that a person engaged in the remembrance of Sri Rama's Name never comes to grief. Those who seek to destroy sins accumulated through crores of births, or to possess untold riches in this world, should constantly and devoutly remember the sweet Name of Sri Rama, the bestower of blessedness."

—*Sri Vyasa*

Though this age of Kali is full of vice, it possesses one great virtue that during this period through mere chanting of the DIVINE NAME one can obtain release from bondage and realise GOD. That which was attained through meditation in Satyayuga, through performance of sacrifices in Tretayuga and through personal service and worship of GOD in Dvaparayuga can be obtained in Kaliyuga through mere chanting of SRI HARI'S NAME.

—*Srimad Bhagavata.*

Ye mortals, do not be terrified by the huge fire of sins blazing before you. It will be extinguished by the shower from the cloudlike Name of GOVINDA.

—*Garuda Purana.*

By worship and meditation or Japa of Mantras the mind is actually *shaped* into the form of the object of worship and is made pure for the time being through the purity of the object (namely, Ishta-Devata) which is its content. By continual practice (Abhyasa) the mind becomes full of the object, to the exclusion of all else, steady in its purity, and does not stray into impurity. So long as the mind exists it must have an object, and the object of Sadhana is to present it with a pure one.

Japa or repetition of the Mantra is compared to the action of a man shaking a sleeper to wake him up.

Sabda or sound exists only where there is motion or Spanda. If there is no Spanda (vibration) there is no Sabda. If there is Sabda there is Spanda (vibration).

'Sabda' which comes from the root *Sabd*,—"to make sound"—ordinarily means sound in general, including that of the voice, word, speech and language. It is either lettered sound (Varnatmaka Sabda) and has a meaning (Artha); that is, it either denotes a thing or connotes the attributes and relations of things; or it is unlettered sound, and is mere Dhvani (Dhvanyatmaka Sabda) such as the sound of a rushing torrent, a clap of thunder, and so forth.

The first vibration which took place at the commencement of creation, that is, on the disturbance of equilibrium (Vaishamyavastha) was a general movement (Samanya-Spanda) in the whole mass of Prakriti. This was the Pranava Dhvani or Om sound. Om is only the approximate representation or gross form of the subtle sound which is heard in Yoga-experience.

A Bija or Seed-Mantra is, strictly speaking, a Mantra of a single letter, such as 'Kam', which is composed of the letter Ka (in Sanskrit) together with the Chandrabindu (ँ) which terminates all Mantras.

The Mantra of a Devata is the form of that Devata. The rhythmical vibrations of its sounds not merely regulate the unsteady vibrations of the sheaths of the worshipper, thus transforming him, but through the power of striving (Sadhanasakti) of the worshipper there arises the form of the Devata which it is.

—*Varnamala*

Of the various kinds of penances in the form of action or austerity, the constant remembrance of Krishna is the best.

The singing of His Name is the best means for the dissolution of various sins, as fire is the best dissolver of metals.

The most heinous sins of men disappear immediately if they remember the Lord even for a moment.

—*Vishnu Purana.*

7. Glory of Rama Nama

(From Ramacharitamanas of Sri Tulasidasji)

बंदउँ नाम राम रघुवर को।। हेतु कृसानु भानु हिमकर को।।
बिधि हरि हरमय बेद प्रान सो। अगुन अनूपम गुन निधान सो।।

1. I worship 'RAMA' the name of Sri Raghunatha. It consists of 'RA', 'AA' and 'MA'. These constitute the roots of Fire, Sun and Moon. ('Ra' is the Bija of fire, 'Aa' is the Bija of the sun and 'Ma' is the Bija of the moon). It is the life-breath of the Vedas. It is formless, incomparable and is the store-house of virtues. These roots ('Ra' 'aa' and 'ma') represent Brahma (the Creator), Vishnu (the Protector) and Siva (the Destroyer) of the world.

महामन्त्र जोइ जपत महेसू। कासी मुकुति हैतु उपदेसू।।
महिमा जासु जान गनराऊ। प्रथम पूजिअत नाम प्रभाऊ।।

2. This is the Mahamantra ever repeated by Lord Siva, who initiates with this Mantra the Jivas who die at Kasi. Lord Ganesa knows the glory of this Name. By the glory of this Name Lord Ganesa is worshipped as the first God in every ceremony.

जान आदिकबि नाम प्रतापू। भयउ सुद्ध करि उलटा जापू॥
सहस नाम सम सुनि सिब बानी। जपि जेई पिय संग भवानी॥

3. Sage Valmiki knows the glory of Rama-Nama. He was purified by a reverse repetition of the same. Parvati recites Rama-Nama along with Siva, knowing that Rama-Nama is equal to 1000 names of the Lord. Once Lord Siva narrated to Parvati the glory of Rama-Nama.

नर नारायण सरिस सुभ्राता। जग पालक बिसेषि जन त्राता॥

4. These two letters 'RA' and 'MA' are like unto Nara and Narayana. They protect the world generally, and particularly the devotee.

राम नाम मनिदीप धरु जीह देहरीं द्वार।
तुलसी भीतर बाहेरहुँ जौं चाहसि उजिआर॥

5. If you want light both inside and outside keep this jewel of Rama-Nama at the door-way of your tongue, says Tulasidasji. If you keep a light on the door you get light both inside and outside. So also Rama-Nama purifies the mind and bestows prosperity on the devotees.

जाना चहहिं गूढ़ गति जेऊ। नाम जीहँ जपि जानहिं तेऊ।
साधक नाम जपहि लय लाएँ। होहिं सिद्ध अनिमादिक पाएँ॥

6. Those who are keen in knowing the supreme Truth, those aspirants after Moksha can attain their objective by repeating Nama. Those who are desirous of eightfold powers (Animadi-Aisvarya) can do so by repeating with earnestness the Names of the Lord.

जपहि नामु जन आरत भारी। मिटहिं कुसंकट होहिं सुखारी॥

7. The afflicted man repeats the Names of the Lord and he is freed from the worst of sufferings.

राम भगत हित नर तनु धारी। सहि संकट किए साधु सुखारी॥
नामु सप्रेम जपत अनयासा। भगत होहि मुद मंगल बासा॥

8. Sri Rama incarnated Himself as a man, underwent untold sufferings to make His devotees (the Devas) happy. But the devotees repeating His Names with devotion cross this ocean of Samsara.

सुक सनकादि सिद्ध मुनि जोगी। नाम प्रसाद ब्रह्मसुख भोगी॥

9. Rishis Suka and Sanaka, perfected sages, enjoy the bliss, Brahmananda, by the power of the Divine Name.

नारद जानेऊ नाम प्रतापू। जग प्रिय हरि हरि हर प्रिय आपू॥

10. "Narada knows the value of Divine Names. Hara (Siva) is dear to Hari. And he (Narada) is dear both to Hara and Hari." The glory of Narada is the glory of the Lord's Name.

8. Change the Drishti

Drishti means vision.

There are four ways of transforming evil into good. He who practises this useful Sadhana will never have an evil Drishti. He will never complain of bad environments. You must put these into practice daily.

1. No man is absolutely bad. Everyone has some good trait or the other. Try to see the good in everyone. Develop the good-finding nature. This will act as a powerful antidote against fault-finding habit.

2. Even a rogue of the first order is a potential saint. He is a saint of the future. Remember this point well. He is not an eternal rogue. Place him in the company of saints. In a moment his pilfering nature will be changed. Hate roguery but not the rogue.

3. Remember that Lord Narayana Himself is acting the part of a rogue, thief and a prostitute in the world's drama. This is His Lila (sporting)—*"Lokavat tu Lila Kaivalyam."* The whole vision becomes changed at once. Devotion arises in your heart immediately when you see a rogue.

4. Have Atma-Drishti everywhere. See Narayana everywhere. Feel His presence. *Vaasudevah Sarvamiti*—Vaasudeva is the All (Gita: VII-19).

5. For a scientist a woman is a mass of electrons. For a Vaiseshika philosopher of Kanada's school of thought, she is a conglomeration of atoms, Paramanus, Dvyanus, Tryanus (two atoms, three atoms). For a tiger she is an object of prey. For a passionate husband, she is an object of enjoyment. For a crying child she is an affectionate mother who will give milk, sweets and other comforts. For a Viveki or a Vairagi, she is a combination of flesh and bone, etc. For a full-blown Jnani, she is Sat-Chit-Ananda Atman—"All is Brahman only."

Change the mental attitude. Then only you will find heaven on earth. What is the earthly use of your reading the Upanishads and the Vedanta-Sutras when you have an evil eye and a foul tongue, my dear comrades?

The first two methods are for beginners. The last three are for advanced students of Yoga. Anyone can combine these five methods, at one time, to his best advantage.

9. Concentration and Meditation

1. "*Desabandhaschittasya dharana*—concentration is fixing the mind on a point external or internal." There can be no concentration without something upon which the mind may rest. A definite purpose, interest, attention will bring success in concentration.

2. The senses draw you out and perturb your peace of mind. If your mind is restless, you cannot make any progress. When the rays of the mind are collected by practice, the mind becomes concentrated and you get Ananda from within. Silence the bubbling thoughts and calm the emotions.

3. You should have patience, adamantine will and untiring persistence. You must be very regular in your practices. Otherwise laziness and adverse forces will take you away from the Lakshya. A well-trained mind can be fixed, at will, upon any object, either inside or outside, to the exclusion of all other thoughts.

4. Everybody possesses some ability to concentrate in some lines. But for spiritual progress, concentration should be developed to a very high degree. A man with an appreciable degree of concentration has more earning capacity and turns out more work in a shorter time. In concentration there should

be no strain on the brain. You should not fight or wrestle with the mind.

5. A man whose mind is filled with passion and all sorts of fantastic desires can hardly concentrate on any object even for a second. Celibacy, Pranayama, reduction of wants and activities, renunciation of sensual objects, solitude, silence, discipline of the senses, annihilation of lust, greed, anger, non-mixing with undesirable persons, giving up of newspaper reading and of visiting cinemas—all increase the power of concentration.

6. Concentration is the only way to get rid of worldly miseries and tribulations. The practitioner will have very good health and a cheerful mental vision. He can get penetrative insight. He can do any work with greater efficiency. Concentration purifies and calms the surging emotions, strengthens the current of thought and clarifies the ideas. Purify the mind first through Yama and Niyama. Concentration without purity is of no use.

7. Japa of any Mantra, and Pranayama will steady the mind, remove Vikshepa and increase the power of concentration. Concentration can be done only if you are free from all distractions. Concentrate on any thing that appeals to you as good or anything which the mind likes best. The mind should be trained to concentrate on gross objects, in the beginning, and later on you can successfully concentrate on subtle objects and abstract ideas. Regularity in practice is of paramount importance.

8. *Gross forms:* Concentrate on a black dot on the wall, a candle-flame, a bright star, moon, the picture of Om, Siva, Rama, Krishna, Devi or any Devata which is your Ishta, in front of you.

9. *Subtle forms:* Sit before the picture of your Ishta-Devata, and close your eyes. Keep a mental picture of your Ishta-Devata at the space between the two eyebrows or in the heart (Anahata-Chakra): concentrate on Muladhara, Ajna or any other internal Chakra; concentrate on divine qualities, such as love, mercy, or any other abstract idea.

10. Twenty Hints on Meditation

1. Have a separate meditation-room under lock and key. Never allow anybody to enter the room. Burn incense there. Wash your feet and then enter the room.

2. Retire to a quiet place or room where you do not fear interruption, so that your mind may feel secure and at rest. Of course, the ideal condition cannot always be obtained, in which case you should do the best you can. You should be alone, yourself, in communion with God or Brahman.

3. Get up at 4 a.m. (Brahmamuhurta) and meditate from 4 a.m. to 6 a.m. Have another sitting at night from 7 p.m. to 8 p.m.

4. Keep a picture of your Ishta-Devata in the room, and also some religious books, the Gita, the Upanishads, the Yoga-Vasishtha, the Bhagavata, etc. Spread your Asana in front of the picture of your Ishta-Devata.

5. Sit on Padma, Siddha, Sukha, or Svastika Asana. Keep the head, neck and trunk in a straight line. Don't bend either forward or backward

6. Close your eyes and concentrate gently on the Trikuti, the space between the two eyebrows. Lock the fingers.

7. Never wrestle with the mind. Do not use any violent effort in concentration. Relax all the muscles and the nerves. Relax the brain. Gently think of your Ishta-Devata. Slowly repeat your Guru-Mantra with Bhava and meaning. Still the bubbling mind. Silence the thoughts.

8. Make no violent effort to control the mind, but rather allow it to run along for a while, and exhaust its efforts. It will take advantage of the opportunity and will jump around like an unchained monkey at first, until it gradually slows down and looks to you for orders. It may take some time to tame the mind, but each time you try it will come around to you in a shorter time.

9. *Saguna and Nirguna Dhyana:* To meditate on a Name and a Form of the Lord is Saguna-Dhyana. This is concrete meditation. Meditate on any Form of God you like, and repeat His Name mentally. This is Saguna-Dhyana. Or, repeat Om mentally and meditate on abstract ideas like Infinity, Eternity,

Purity, Consciousness, Truth, Bliss, etc., identifying these with your Self. This is Nirguna-Dhyana. Stick to one method. In the initial stages, Saguna-Dhyana alone is suitable for the vast majority of persons.

10. Again and again withdraw the mind from worldly objects when it runs away from the Lakshya, and fix it there. This sort of combat will go on for some months.

11. When you meditate on the Lord Vishnu; in the beginning, keep His picture in front of you. Look at it with steady gazing, without winking the eyelids. See His feet first, then the yellow silken robe, then the ornaments around His neck, then His face, earrings, crown, the head, set with diamonds, then His armlets on bracelets, then His conch, disc, mace and lotus. Then come again to the feet. Now start again the same process. Do this again and again for half an hour. When you feel tired look steadily on the face only. Do this practice for three months.

12. Then close your eyes and mentally visualise the picture and rotate the mind in the different parts, as you did before.

13. You can associate the attributes of God, as omnipotence, omniscience, purity, perfection, etc., during the course of your meditation.

14. If evil thoughts enter your mind, do not use your will-force in driving them. You will only lose your energy. You will only tax your will. You will fatigue yourself. The greater the efforts you make, the more the evil thoughts will return with redoubled force. They will return more quickly, also. The thoughts will become more powerful. Be indifferent. Keep quiet. They will pass away soon. Or, substitute good counter thoughts (Pratipaksha-Bhavana method). Or think of the picture of God and the Mantra, again and again, forcibly. Or pray.

15. Never let a day pass without meditation. Be regular and systematic. Take Sattvic food. Fruits and milk will help mental focussing. Give up meat, fish, eggs, smoking, liquors, etc.

16. Dash cold water on the face to drive off drowsiness. Stand up for 15 minutes. Tie the tuft of hair on the head, with a piece of string to a nail above. As soon as you begin to doze,

the string will pull you up, will wake you up. It will serve the part of a mother. Or lean upon an improvised swing, for 10 minutes, and move yourself to and fro. Do 10 or 20 mild Kumbhakas (Pranayamas). Do Sirshasana and Mayurasana. Take only milk and fruits at night. By these methods you can combat sleep.

17. Be careful in the selection of your companions. Give up going to talkies. Talk a little. Observe Mouna for two hours daily. Do not mix with undesirable persons. Read good, inspiring, religious books. (This is negative good company, if you do not get positive good company). Have Satsanga. These are all auxiliaries to meditation.

18. Do not shake the body. Keep it as firm as a rock. Breathe slowly. Do not stretch the body every now and then. Have the right mental attitude as taught by your Guru.

19. When the mind is tired, do not concentrate. Give it a little rest.

20. When an idea exclusively occupies the mind, it is transformed into an actual physical or mental state. Therefore if you keep the mind fully occupied with the thought of God alone, you will get into Nirvikalpa Samadhi very quickly. Therefore exert in right earnest.

Course of Sadhana

1. You must be able to sit in one Asana, with head erect, for a period of at least 3 hours at a stretch.

2. Practise Pranayama for half an hour daily.

3. You must get up at 4 a.m. and start meditation first. Then you can have the practice of Asana and Pranayama. Meditation is the most important Sadhana.

4. Have concrete meditation at first. To begin with, meditate on any form you like best. Feel the Indwelling Presence in that form and think of the attributes—Purity, Perfection, All-pervading Intelligence, Absolute Bliss, Omnipotence, etc. When the mind runs again and again, bring it to the point. Have another sitting for meditation at night. Be regular in your practice.

5. Develop right thinking, right feeling, right acting and right speaking.

6. Eradicate vicious qualities, such as anger, lust, greed, egoism, hatred, etc.

7. Discipline the Indriyas. Observe the vow of silence for two hours daily.

8. Develop virtues—forgiveness, mercy, love, kindness, patience, perseverance, courage, truthfulness, etc.

9. Keep a daily spiritual diary, regularly, and stick to your daily spiritual routine at all costs.

10. Write your Ishta-Mantra 'Hari Om', 'Sri Rama', 'Om Namo Narayanaya', 'Om Namo Bhagavate Vaasudevaya', 'Om Namah Sivaya', etc., in a notebook, for one hour daily.

11. Be a pure vegetarian.

Mantras of Sri Dattatreya

ॐ श्रीदत्तात्रेयाय नमः। ॐ नमो भगवते दत्तात्रेयाय।

Om Sri Dattatreyaya Namah. Om Namo Bhagavate Dattatreyaya

ॐ द्रां ॐ नमः श्रीगुरुदेवाय परमपुरुषाय
सर्वदेवतावशीकराय सर्वारिष्टविनाशाय
सर्वदुर्मन्त्रच्छेदनाय त्रैलोक्यं वशमानय स्वाहा ॐ द्रां ॐ।

Om Draam Om Namah Sri Gurudevaya Paramapurushaya Sarvadevatavaseekaraya Sarvarishta-vinasanaya Sarvaodurmantrachhedanaya Trailokyam Vasamanaya Svaha Om Draam Om.

11. Mantra-Writing

Mantra-Writing Leads to Meditation

Of the various methods of Japa described in the scriptures, Mantra-writing is the most efficacious. It helps the aspirant in concentrating the mind and gradually leads to meditation.

Benefits

1. *Concentration*—Distractions are minimised, as the mind, tongue, hands and eyes are all engaged in the Mantra.

This increases the power of concentration and efficiency in work.

2. *Control*—The mind is controlled by the power of Mantra and it will work better and quicker for you.

3. *Evolution*—Due to repeated innumerable impacts of the Mantra on the subconscious mind, subtle, spiritual impressions are made, which hasten the soul's progress in evolution.

4. *Peace*—If you are disturbed due to worries or untoward incidents, the mind will get calm and peaceful.

5. *Force*—A mighty spiritual force is generated in course of time, in the atmosphere of the place where you write Mantras or keep notebooks. It helps in secular and spiritual progress.

Conclusion—Begin today. Do not procrastinate. Give it a sincere trial. Be a master of your mind, not its slave. Write the Mantra on one to three pages a day. Follow the rules, as far as possible, if you want quicker spiritual progress.

Rules for Mantra-writing

1. Select a Mantra, or Name of God, and write it with ink in a notebook, daily, in any script, on 1 to 3 pages.

2. Sit in the same place at the same time, daily. If it is a room, and if possible, keep it under lock and key.

3. Write after a bath or after washing hands, feet, face and mouth.

4. Sit in one pose throughout. Do not move till you complete the day's writing.

5. Observe silence and avoid talks, engagements or calls.

6. Fix the eyes on the notebook. Do not move till it is completed.

7. Repeat the Mantra or the Name mentally while writing.

8. Fix the mind on the form and attributes of the Lord, while writing the Name or the Mantra.

9. Adopt one uniform system of writing, from top to bottom or from left to right.

10. Write each Mantra or Name completely, at a time, and not in parts.

11. Do not change the Mantra or the Name. Select one and stick to it for life.

12. Preserve the completed Mantra-writing notebooks, near your place of worship.

12. Instructions to Aspirants During Mantra-Initiation

1. In this Kali Yuga God-realisation can easily be attained through Japa and Kirtan. Have faith in this.

2. Remember saints like Sage Narada, Lord Gauranga, Tukaram, Valmiki, Mira Bai and others who attained the Godhead through Nama-Smarana.

3. To receive initiation of the Bhagavan-Nama from a Guru is a great blessing. The Mantra-Chaitanya, the power hidden in the Mantra, is easily awakened.

4. Have regular sittings for Japa—in the morning and evening. Brahmamuhurta is the best period for Japa. Get up at 4 a.m. and do Japa for two hours.

5. Make it a point to do at least three Maalas of Japa (1 Maala is 108 repetitions); gradually increase the number.

6. Repeat the Name mentally throughout the day.

7. Offer the Japa to God—Isvararpana.

13. Mantras for Fulfilment of Wishes and for Cure

Mantra for Attaining Success

ॐ कृष्ण कृष्ण महायोगिन् भक्तानामभयंकर।
गोविन्द परमानन्द सर्वं मे वशमानय॥

O Krishna! O Krishna! O great Yogin! O bestower of fearlessness on (Thy) devotees! O Govinda! O Supreme Bliss! Bring everything in my favour (under my control).

Mantra for Attaining Prosperity

ॐ आयुर्देहि धनं देहि विद्यां देहि महेश्वरि।
समस्तमखिलं देहि देहि मे परमेश्वरि॥

Give me long life; give me wealth; give me knowledge, O Mahesvari! Give me everything, O Paramesvari! Give all things in plenty.

Mantra for Getting a Son

(सन्तानगोपालमन्त्रः)

ॐ देवकीसुत गोविन्द वासुदेव जगत्पते।
देहि मे तनयं कृष्ण त्वामहं शरणं गतः* ॥

O son of Devaki! O Govinda! O Vaasudeva! O Lord of the Universe! O Krishna! Give me a son; I have taken refuge in Thee.

Note: Repeat this Mantra 32 lakh times, or at least one lakh times. Do the Japa after your morning ablutions. After finishing the total number of Japa, consult a Pandit and perform Havan. Feed Brahmins, Sadhus and the poor, according to your means, and distribute clothes and give Dakshina to them.

Mantra for Relief from Pain Caused by Scorpion-sting

ॐ देवदानवयुद्धे तु मथ्यमाने महोदधौ।
जातोऽसि वृश्चिराजस्त्वं स्वगृहं गच्छ महाविष ॥

In the fight between the Devas and Danavas (Rakshasas), when the great ocean was being churned, O Vrischikaraja (king of scorpions), thou emanated (from it). O one with great poison! Go (back) to thy own abode.

Note: Tie a piece of cloth where the pain of the sting is too much. Repeat the above Mantra a number of times. Now untie the cloth and wave it against the air (a gesture to show that the poison has gone away). Continue this routine 8 or 10 times. He who repeats this Mantra at least 108 times a day or who has already attained Siddhi of this Mantra will be endowed with the gift of cure.

*It is to be recited by the wife it will be गता

A Panacea for Snake-bite

यो जरत्कारुणा जातो जरत्कारौ महायशाः।
आस्तीकः सर्पसत्रे वः पन्नगान् योऽभ्यरक्षत।
तं स्मरन्तं महाभागा न मां हिंसितुमर्हथ॥

Yo jaratkaruna jato jaratkarau mahayasah;
Aastikah sarpasatre vah pannagan yoabhyarakshata;
Tam smarantam mahabhaga na mam himsitumarhata.

The glorious Aastika was born of Rishi Jaratkaru and Nagakanya Jaratkaru. He protected you, serpents, from falling into the snake-sacrifice. O great serpents! I think of him. Do not bite me.

सर्पापसर्प भद्रं ते गच्छ सर्प महाविष।
जनमेजययज्ञान्ते आस्तीकवचनं स्मर॥

Sarpapasarpa bhadram te gachha sarpa mahavisha;
Janamejaya-yajnante Aastikavachanam smara.

O serpent, having terrible poison, go away. May there be auspiciousness unto you. Go away. Think over what Aastika said at the end of the snake-sacrifice.

आस्तीकस्य वचः श्रुत्वा यः सर्पो न निवर्तते।
शतधा भिद्यते मूर्ध्नि शिंशावृक्षफलं यथा॥

Aastikasya vachah srutva yah sarpo na nivartate;
Satadha bhidyate murdhni simsavriksha-phalam yatha.

The head of the serpent which does not return on hearing the people mention the word Aastika will burst into a hundred pieces like the fruit of the Simsa tree.

Any one who reads and does Japa of the above Slokas, either in the morning or evening, will have no fear from snakes.

King Parikshit died being bitten by the serpent Takshaka. So, his son, Janamejaya, performed a snake-sacrifice to destroy all snakes in the world. Aastika was the son of Jaratkaru, the sister of Takshaka. He came and stopped the snake-sacrifice in the middle. So the snakes are bound in duty to respect his name. For fuller particulars please refer to Adiparva of the Mahabharata.

SADHANA TATTVA

OR

THE SCIENCE OF SEVEN CULTURES

For Quick Evolution of the Human Soul

INTRODUCTION

(a) An ounce of practice is better than tons of theory. Practise Yoga, Religion and Philosophy in daily life and attain Self-realisation.

(b) These thirty-two instructions give the essence of the Eternal Religion (Sanatana Dharma) in its purest form. They are suitable for modern busy householders with fixed hours of work. Modify them to suit your convenience and increase the period gradually.

(c) In the beginning take only a few practicable resolves which form a small but definite advance over your present habits and character. In case of ill-health, pressure of work or unavoidable engagements replace your active Sadhana by frequent remembrance of God.

HEALTH CULTURE

1. Eat moderately. Take light and simple food. Offer it to God before you eat. Have a balanced diet.

2. Avoid chillies, garlic, onions, tamarind, etc., as far as possible. Give up tea, coffee, smoking, betels, meat and wine entirely.

3. Fast on Ekadasi days. Take milk, fruits or roots only.

4. Practise Yoga Asanas or physical exercises for fifteen to thirty minutes every day. Take a long walk or play some vigorous games daily.

ENERGY CULTURE

5. Observe silence (Mouna) for two hours daily and four to eight hours on Sundays.

6. Observe celibacy according to your age and circumstances. Restrict the indulgence to once a month. Decrease it gradually to once a year. Finally take a vow of abstinence for whole life.

ETHICAL CULTURE

7. Speak the TRUTH. Speak little. Speak kindly. Speak sweetly.

8. Do not injure anyone in thought, word or deed. Be kind to all.

9. Be sincere, straightforward and open-hearted in your talks and dealings.

10. Be honest. Earn by the sweat of your brow. Do not accept any money, things or favour unless earned lawfully. Develop nobility and integrity.

11. Control fits of anger by serenity, patience, love, mercy and tolerance. Forget and forgive. Adapt yourself to men and events.

WILL CULTURE

12. Live without sugar for a week or month. Give up salt on Sundays.

13. Give up cards, novels, cinemas and clubs. Fly from evil company. Avoid discussions with materialists. Do not mix with persons who have no faith in God or who criticise your Sadhana.

14. Curtail your wants. Reduce your possessions. Have plain living and high thinking.

HEART CULTURE

15. Doing good to others is the highest religion. Do some selfless service for a few hours every week, without egoism or expectation of reward. Do your worldly duties in the same spirit. Work is worship. Dedicate it to God.

16. Give two to ten per cent of your income in charity every month. Share what you have with others. Let the world be your family. Remove selfishness.

17. Be humble and prostrate yourself to all beings mentally. Feel the Divine Presence everywhere. Give up vanity, pride and hypocrisy.

18. Have unwavering faith in God, the Gita and your Guru. Make a total self-surrender to God and pray: "Thy Will be done; I want nothing." Submit to the Divine Will in all events and happenings with equanimity.

19. See God in all beings and love them as your own Self. Do not hate anyone.

20. Remember God at all times or, at least, on rising from bed, during a pause in work and before going to bed. Keep a Maala in your pocket.

PSYCHIC CULTURE

21. Study one chapter or ten to twenty-five verses of the Gita with meaning, daily. Learn Sanskrit, at least sufficient to understand the Gita in original.

22. Memorise the whole of the Gita, gradually. Keep it always in your pocket.

23. Read the Ramayana, Bhagavata, Upanishads, Yoga-Vasishtha or other religious books daily or on holidays.

24. Attend religious meetings, Kirtans and Satsanga of saints at every opportunity. Organise such functions on Sundays or holidays.

25. Visit a temple or place of worship at least once a week and arrange to hold Kirtans or discourses there.

26. Spend holidays and leave-periods, when possible, in the company of saints or practise Sadhana at a holy place in seclusion.

SPIRITUAL CULTURE

27. Go to bed early. Get up at four o'clock. Answer calls of nature, clean your mouth and take a bath.

28. Recite some prayers and Kirtan Dhvanis. Practise Pranayama, Japa and meditation from five to six o'clock. Sit on Padma, Siddha, or Sukha Asana throughout, without movement, by gradual practice.

29. Perform your daily Sandhya, Gayatri Japa, Nityakarma and worship, if any.

30. Write your favourite Mantra or Name of God in a notebook for ten to thirty minutes, daily.

31. Sing the Names of God (Kirtan), prayers, Stotras and Bhajans for half to one hour at night with family and friends.

32. Make annual resolves on the above lines. Regularity, tenacity and fixity are essential. Record your Sadhana in a spiritual diary daily. Review it every month and correct your failures.